other books by J. Z. Colby:

The NEBADOR series of young-adult science fiction novels

the incredible journey of five young adults from poverty and oppression to respected citizenship in the wide universe

Book One: The Test
Book Two: Journey
Book Three: Selection
Book Four: Flight Training
Book Five: Back to the Stars
Book Six: Star Station
2012
Book Seven: The Local Universe
2013
Book Eight: Witness
2014

Standing on Your Own Two Feet

Young Adults Surviving 2012 and Beyond

by J. Z. Colby

dealing with little, everyday things like:
economic collapse
climate change
resource depletion
civil unrest
war
famine

Nebador Archives

Cover art and illustrations by Rachael Hedges

Editorial assistance by Alex Chalcraft, Tim Kutscha,
    Cecelia Harper, June Nishihara, and
    Rachael Hedges

For other editions (print and ebook), and updates in
the author's Youth Futures blog, please see:

www.nebador.com

Ν Α

Nebador Archives
Kelso, Washington, USA

Library of Congress Control Number: 2012900109
Manufactured in the USA

ISBN: 978-1-936253-46-3
TWOFEET2012PBG1: paperback global edition,
    6" x 9", 160 pages, medium print
    (12-point Georgia type), revision 1

Greetings, young people of planet Earth,

This book is a gift to you. It is a small effort on my part to do something about the shame I feel because adults are handing you a world in worse shape than we found it.

We were warned. All during the 1960s and 1970s, scientists and scholars warned us that we were starting to damage our environment, and that we would soon run short of energy and other resources. Oil production in the USA peaked in the early 1970s, and we had our first "energy crisis." I was 15 then, the age of the two main characters in the story part of this book.

Our civilization could have changed course at that time. We could have decided to quit harming the environment with air and water pollution, and get used to the fact that energy and mineral resources wouldn't remain cheap and plentiful forever. Instead, our leaders of all kinds (political, social, financial, religious, etc.) decided to do nothing and pretend we could keep on "growing" forever on a small, fragile planet.

That was the biggest mistake of all of human history to date. Hopefully this little book will help some of you survive and be happy in the coming years. I will be with you for as long as I can, as a helper, but your time to lead is almost here.

J. Z. Colby
2012

Contents

Jumping In 1

Just Frozen Water 2

Your Go-Bag 4

Ashley's "Team" 6

Go-Bag Details 8

Girl Stuff 10

Boy Stuff 12

Murphy's Law 14

Jeremy's Pantry 16

Shallow/Deep Pantry . 18

Food Basics 20

What's the Fuss? 22

Rosemary's Go-Bag 24

End of the World? 26

Rosemary's Mistake 28

Letting Go 30

A Strange Enemy 32

Essential First-Aid 34

First-Aid Class 36

Beyond First-Aid 38

Drugs and Blades! 40

Your Parents? 42

What do we NEED? 44

Your Web of Life 46

Ashley's Web 48

Happiness 50

Get Real 52

Buying Stuff 54

Jeremy's "Firearm" 56

Emotional Resilience .. 58

Bobby Coming of Age . 60

Our Myths 62

Black or White? 64

Money Without Jobs ... 66

Ashley's Job 68

Community 70

Ashley's Pay 72

Your Skills 74

Dangerous! 76

Invisibility 78

Invisibility Ideas 80

Like a Super-Hero 82

More Invisibility 84
Lifeboat Ethics 86
EROEI 88
Our Place in History ... 90
The Future 92
Sleep-Walking? 94
Shoveling Bull 96
Our Leaders? 98
Meeting Places 100
Dog Poop 102
Your Money 104
Banks 106
Not Banks 108
Out of Debt! 110
Wheels 112
Wealth! 114
Can Money Die? 116
Rosemary's Wealth ... 118
Home Sweet Home? ..120

Bad News? 122
Voluntary Poverty 124
Angel or Reptile? 126
Good Boundaries 128
Not Your Business! ... 130
Reality Levels 132
Is This a Test? 134
Lullabies 136
To Be Refugee? 138
Religion 140
Public Education? 142
Ashley's Path 144
Medicine 146
New Team Members? 148
Your Growing Team ..150
A Team of 5? 152
Farewell to the Team .154
Closing Thoughts 156
Master Checklist 158

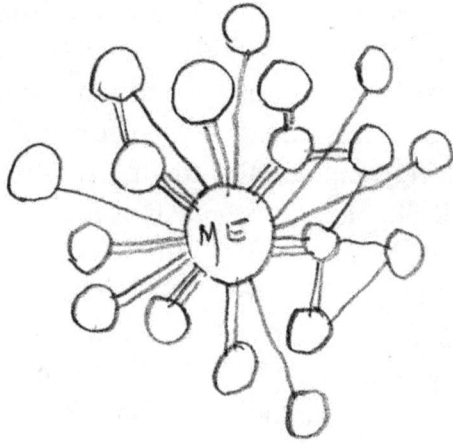

"Personal Power is the ability to stand on your own two feet, with a smile on your face, in the middle of a universe that contains a million ways to crush you."

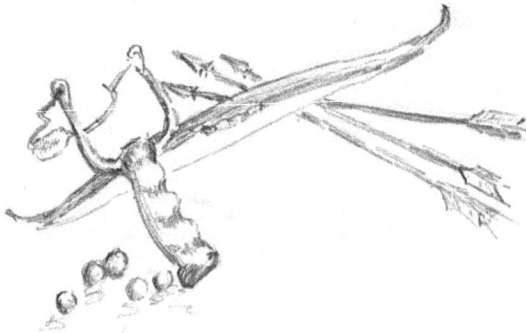

Jumping In

We'll talk, as we go, about how and why bad things are happening in the world, but since this book is mostly about *getting ready* while you have time, we'll jump right into a project that could save your butt in many situations.

Sometimes the things I suggest won't be "cool" or "politically correct." Too bad. Time is short. You've got lots to think about, learn about, make decisions about, and scrape up, before you'll be even *half-way* ready for the stuff that's lurking in our future.

I'm not going to waste much time trying to convince you that economic collapse, climate change, civil unrest, resource depletion, war, famine, and all that stuff, are right around the corner. It would take too long, and frankly, if you haven't seen the signs already, you're probably one of those people who refuses to get ready until it's too late.

But since you're reading this book, you've got your eyes wide open, right?

Just Frozen Water

The inter-city train had barely left the 243rd Street Station when the freezing rain started. Ashley pressed her face against the window and could see cars starting to slide around on the streets.

With her old, tattered daypack nestled in her lap, Ashley smiled. Her mom had begged her to take the new one she had just received for her 15th birthday, bright pink and glittery. Ashley had stood her ground. The new one would be her school bag, not her go-bag.

Horns and a crashing noise penetrated the electric train's soft sounds, and Ashley rubbed the fog off the window. Cars and trucks were piling up on the freeway, and more were coming behind, unable to stop.

Ashley took a deep breath and smiled, glad she had taken the train instead of accepting the ride her aunt had offered.

Just then the train's interior lights started flickering, and a moment later, the train coasted to a stop. Many voices around Ashley showed frustration, fear, even a little anger.

"Sorry folks," the driver's voice came over the speakers, "the ice is coating the wires. They'll have a bus here as soon as they can."

Ashley looked out the window, saw streets coated with black ice and cars in the ditch, and shook her head.

She opened her bag, pulled out sturdy walking shoes and wool socks, and slipped her sandals in. The hood of her coat brought comfort as the temperature in the train started to drop. Finally, she ripped open a Power Bar, stood up, and pressed the door release.

Several people grumbled about the blast of cold air that entered the train. One woman shrieked, "Don't go out there! It's dangerous!"

As the doors closed behind her, Ashley took a deep breath of the cold, fresh air, and felt completely alive. She knew the streets and sidewalks would be slippery, but the bike path had grass or gravel on the sides that would give her traction.

"Let's go, feet!" she said, and headed for home.

Your Go-Bag

Ashley is the person, but the story you just read is about her go-bag. It's not just any bag. It was carefully chosen and packed after reading a book like this, finding friends who also wanted to be prepared, and doing some experimenting. The contents are very special to Ashley, and anyone who touches it risks her wrath. It's very personal, and in a very real sense, is a magic bag.

You need one too, and you need it *now*. Most of you already have something that will work, an old daypack or shoulder bag, so now you need to get serious about what's in it.

Phone, make-up, games — those are toys, things to play with, everyone has them. They're add-ons for the occasion, not the essential contents of your go-bag.

"Isn't a phone important for emergencies?" you ask. True, it can sometimes help, but it's too vulnerable to power failure and system overload.

This book is *not* about those little personal emergencies when you're the only one in trouble and the whole world (parents, police, fire trucks, and ambulances) can rush to your rescue. This is about those times when *lots of people* are affected, the phone and emergency systems are overloaded, and your parents can't get to you. This book is about taking care of yourself for a while, and doing what needs to be done for yourself and those with you.

Imagine the family car breaks down 10 miles from anything. You're not 2 anymore, and your parents can't carry you.

Imagine the credit-card system goes down (it's just phone lines or internet), you're hungry, and no one brought any real money.

Imagine a bad storm knocks down poles and wires, blocks roads, and forces you to spend the night under a tree.

Your go-bag is your magic tool bag, ready to provide for you in a wide variety of situations. It's also a time machine. Emergencies all have one thing in common: you *cannot* prepare for them when they happen. You prepare before, or you're screwed. Your go-bag lets you prepare *before* stuff happens, in your house, with the heat and lights on.

Ashley's "Team"

"I had blisters on my blisters!" Ashley moaned as she finished her story.

Jeremy poked at the campfire with a stick, then tossed it in to give more light. "Were your parental units freaked out?"

"Of course. That's their purpose in life. They kept asking me why I didn't get on the express bus, and I had to tell them *three times* that I was walking twice as fast as the traffic on the freeway."

"I heard all the roads were like skating rinks until this morning," 12-year-old Rosemary said timidly, hugging her knees.

"Totally!" Ashley continued. "Then my dad said that if I wouldn't use my phone in an emergency, I shouldn't have one. Before I could say anything, the news came on, saying that mobile phone service was *starting* to be restored. He dropped the subject."

Bobby, the youngest at 11, chuckled. "Did you have everything you needed? Sometimes, at the mall ... you know ... you spend your emergency money ..."

Ashley squirmed. "I know. It burns a hole in my bag. My Power Bar got me home, but barely. I ate two huge sandwiches at about midnight while my parents grilled me. Next time I earn some money, I'm gonna seal it in plastic before I put it in my go-bag!"

Her three friends laughed.

✳

Preparing to deal with stuff is a lot easier, and a lot more fun, with friends. But you must be careful — friends who will stand at your side through thick and thin might be different people than the ones you like to hang out with at the mall.

Ashley's team does not include her parents. They are neutral, not stopping her from preparing, but not really understanding. Some of you have parents who can be on your team, and others may have to do it completely without adult help.

In this story, three friends have joined Ashley, all of them fairly smart, strong, and loyal. They all have their eyes open wide, see big problems coming, and don't want to be crushed. To Ashley's surprise, only one person on her team was about her age, and Jeremy wasn't a boy she had ever considered liking.

Go-Bag Details

It's a daypack or shoulder bag, easy to grab, easy to carry. It should be sturdy, but look kind of old and tired. If it screams "Rich Kid," thieves will take notice. Bright and flashy is bad if you need to slip through the shadows to avoid trouble. Black, dark blue, brown ...

In the bottom are walking shoes or boots, unless they're on your feet. Wool socks are best, plus a spare pair. Cold, wet feet can kill.

Money and ID are in a wallet, little purse, or small fanny pack so you can pull it out quickly if you need to leave your go-bag somewhere, like at the cashier while shopping. Also in the wallet/purse are your important phone numbers and addresses. Your "address book" in your phone or on the internet won't be there when you need it most.

You've got two kinds of money: spending and emergency. Your emergency money depends on how much it costs to get home from the places you go, if your usual rides can't help. Minimum, in the USA, is 5 good $1 bills, 4 good $5 bills, and 4 quarters, total $26. "Good" bills because vending and ticket machines can be picky.

A hoodie or winter coat may not fit *inside* your go-bag, but should always be with it. This item will change with the seasons. Even in the summer, it can get pretty cool at 3:00am. (That's right, you need to be ready for 3:00am. It happens every day.)

This list is what responsible people need in the real world. It's not for school, airplanes, or other high-security areas (HSAs) without modification.

Wallet/purse — money, ID, address book (Ziploc
   bag to keep it dry)
Pocket knife/can opener — remove for all HSAs,
   illegal in a very few places
Flashlight — small, remove for airplanes
Toiletries — comb, tissue, tampons, ...
Food — "Power Bars" or whatever
Water/juice bottle — remove for airplanes
City/county map(s) — based on where you go
Sun and snow hats — both, all year long
First-Aid kit — small, for cuts, burns
Glasses? — in a hard case
Medicines? — in original containers, remove for
   school
Coat — changes with the seasons, may not fit inside

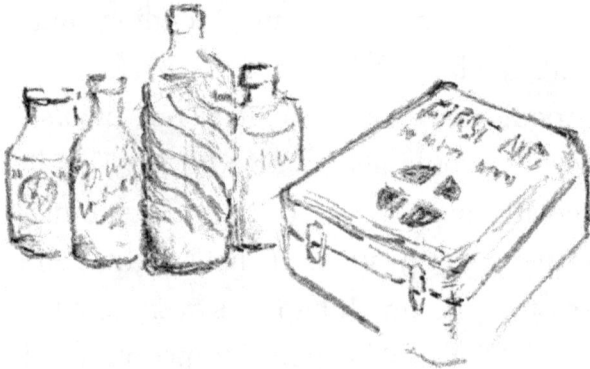

Girl Stuff

After carefully applying a bead of mustard to her golden-brown hot dog, Ashley devoured it in several bites, then reached for her bag. "That day when we had the ice storm, that was the *last* day I only had *one* Power Bar in my go-bag. And I thought on the way home that I *could* have had two or three unprepared friends with me. What would I have done *then?*"

Out of Ashley's go-bag came a cloth sack with eight Power Bars inside, several different flavors. But Ashley wasn't finished.

"And you wouldn't *believe* how thirsty I got on the way home, and no, you can't get a drink by opening your mouth and letting a few bits of frozen rain hit your tongue. I tried!"

Two small bottles of apple juice emerged. "I used to carry an empty water bottle. I thought, *why carry extra weight until I need it.* I learned. When you need it, it's *too late to get it!*"

All three of Ashley's friends chuckled.

"But I've *always* had this ..."

She pulled out a small first aid kit and opened it. "This is my pride and joy. It's not quite enough for open heart surgery ..."

Rosemary giggled.

"... but it's got antibiotic powder, compresses, butterflies, tape, and everything else for wounds, burn gel and wrap, calcium tablets and vitamin C, antiseptic packets and breathing masks, the works!"

Bobby was peering into the box with keen interest. "We should know this stuff, shouldn't we?"

Ashley nodded. "If you want to live ... and keep your friends alive."

Rosemary shuddered. Jeremy was paying attention, but didn't look thrilled.

"Will you teach us?" Bobby asked. "And help us make kits like yours?"

Ashley nodded vigorously. "But there's one thing in *my* go-bag that you boys won't want to be caught *dead* with!"

Rosemary giggled as Ashley dangled a small package of tampons.

Boy Stuff

Bobby was fascinated with the stuff Jeremy pulled from his go-bag. Ashley and Rosemary sat quietly.

Jeremy opened a small canvas pouch to reveal a stainless steel tool that folded open to become pliers and wire cutters. Out of the handles came screw drivers, can and bottle openers, knife blades, and even a small saw. A dozen little tool tips peeked out of slots in the canvas, ready to fit just about any screw in the world. A tiny adjustable wrench completed the set.

"My dad has a big tool box," Jeremy explained, "but he usually forgets to put it in the car when we go places. This little baby got us going once last summer when we were way out in the woods and the car wouldn't start. I think that's when my dad realized I was growing up."

"Cool!" Bobby said with admiration, mentally putting a similar tool on his wish-list.

Next came a plastic case, out of which slid an old calculator. "I found this in a thrift store. Completely solar, and they don't make them anymore because people complained they couldn't use them in the dark."

Rosemary laughed. Ashley pretended to play a tiny violin.

"Has all the trig functions, pi, everything."

Bobby grinned. Ashley's eyes glazed over.

Finally, three thin books emerged. "I don't always keep these in my go-bag," Jeremy explained.

Bobby picked up *Basic Auto Mechanics*, and Rosemary glanced at *Bicycle Repair*.

The third book caught Ashley's eye, and she struggled to read its title aloud. "Epitome ... of the Pharma ... copeia and National Formulary." She looked at Jeremy.

He cringed slightly. "It's from the 1950s. All about herbs and simple chemicals and stuff. I don't know much about it yet, but I have a hunch we're gonna need to know that stuff someday."

Ashley shrugged, but for some reason, couldn't get the little book out of her mind for the rest of the evening.

Murphy's Law

"If anything can go wrong, it will, and at the worst possible time."

This "law" comes in many different forms, all about the same. It's a law like in math or physics, describing how the universe appears to work. It was "written" by God or Nature (whichever you prefer), and not by people.

Some people think that if you prepare for bad things, you'll attract them into your life. If you believe that, you don't need this book. Just don't whine if bad things come knocking anyway.

A much better attitude: "Hope for the best, and

prepare for the worst."

Why?

The price of preparing for something that doesn't happen is very low: a little money for supplies, a few hours to read a book, and practicing enough to be comfortable with your new gear.

The price of *not* preparing for something that *does* happen can be very high: an untreated illness or injury, becoming a refugee, even death.

Risk = Probability x Severity

Don't worry, no math required. We'll just break this down into some different possibilities:

High probability, low severity — About lunchtime, every day, you'll get hungry. Preparation is easy: pack a lunch, or take lunch money.

Low probability, high severity — An asteroid could hit the Earth. No preparation possible. Brush it off, and enjoy life, however long it lasts.

Medium probability, medium severity — This is where we all need to do some work. This stuff is just likely enough, especially today, that it'll probably happen to you if you keep your head in the sand. And it's just bad enough that you'll *really* regret not preparing. But it's also just hard enough that you *won't* prepare if you're lazy. That's what this book is all about, but *you* have to decide.

Jeremy's Pantry

"Whew!" Jeremy breathed as he plopped down on a log.

"What's up?" Ashley asked as she carefully placed little twigs over a burning wad of newspaper.

"It took more than a month, but I *finally* talked my parents into letting me make a ... what did the book call it? ... a deep pantry. But it all has to go in my *bedroom*. It's gonna look like a grocery store!"

Rosemary giggled and handed more sticks to Ashley.

"Hey!" Bobby jumped in with an idea. "That way, you can charge high prices when your dad's unemployment insurance runs out and they come knocking!"

Jeremy laughed. "I wish! By then, they'll forget it was my idea. Nobody thinks that far ahead in my family."

"My mom's the same way," Rosemary moaned.

"Thinks her temp job will last forever."

Bobby snickered. "My mom just lost hers. How much you gonna spend on food?" he asked, looking at Jeremy.

"I'm working for Mrs. Green now on Thursdays, so I'm making almost $50 a week. My dad's starting to get jealous. He keeps putting in applications, but no luck. I still want to get a silver dime or two, but the rest will go to my pantry, except for a few dollars to play with. My brother and sister both think I'm crazy."

Ashley grinned. "They might change their minds when they get hungry."

＊

Your go-bag was easy to make, and easy to keep secret. It just looks like any kid's daypack.

But a deep pantry could easily trigger prejudice and fear in other people. While the good times continue, it'll just be "weird." If bad times arrive for your family or community, people who didn't prepare usually vent their frustrations at people who did, and call them "hoarders." When people get hungry, the rules of civilization are quickly forgotten.

So, you should expect to have to share your deep pantry, or it will just be taken from you by force. But in the process, you can build new family or community relationships by asking for something in return.

Shallow/Deep Pantry

Most homes have food for about a week on the shelves and in the refrigerator, maybe 2 weeks. This is called a "shallow pantry." Add a couple of unprepared neighbors, take away electricity, gas, or both, and you'd probably be lucky if your shallow pantry lasted a week.

If you want to change this situation, you'll have to have a serious talk with your parents. They may be able to provide money, but not time, to the creation of a "deep pantry." Maybe neither. Storage space is an issue in many houses. The closet in your bedroom may have to help out.

Depending on who's in your family, and who else wanders through, your "deep pantry" may have to be limited to boring things that no one will snitch: dried beans, flour, corn meal, powdered milk, and other "staple foods."

In any case, a "deep pantry" is all non-perishable stuff. Refrigerated and frozen foods are too vulnerable to power failures. As you decide what to get, be serious — there's about a hundred times as much food in a bag of flour as in a bag of chips. And don't forget the other things needed to make food edible: if you get flour, you also need oil and baking powder.

You can't cook or wash without water. Drinking and cooking water can be easily stored in plastic jugs, 1 quart or liter per person per day, minimum, but 2 is better. Washing takes a lot more, but it doesn't have to be as clean (stream, river, lake).

If your cooking fuel is electricity or piped gas, you need an alternate: bottled gas, fireplace, wood stove.

In the process of making a deep pantry, you'll learn about "shelf life." Nothing lasts forever. The "expiration dates" printed on packages are conservative, and most things last much longer. Refrigeration, or at least an unheated room, greatly increases shelf life.

A thick plastic bag is important for anything that comes in paper, like flour and sugar. Heat, moisture, and insects are the enemies. Most mixes and prepared foods contain oil or fat, which goes rancid quickly (1-2 years). Rancidity is dangerous, but simple "staleness" is not.

✳

<u>Wet canned food, flour, oil, dry milk</u> 2-5 years
<u>Dry canned food, whole grains</u> 10-50 years
<u>Honey, sugar, salt, wheat berries</u> almost forever

Food Basics

Can you recognize food when you see it, and if you're hungry, eat it?

It's a serious question. Many modern people can't. Imagine that you come home from school or work one day, open the cupboards and refrigerator, and find a bag of rock-hard wheat berries, a bowl of dirty turnip roots from the garden, and a dead chicken (feathers, guts, and all).

You could yell, "Mom! There's nothing to eat!"

Dead silence. No one else is home. Your stomach starts to growl. You find a note that says no one else *will* be home until tomorrow. The nearest grocery store is 5 miles away. What are you going to do?

Okay, you know in your heart now if you're prepared to recognize, prepare, and eat basic foods. I won't bore you with the details of making a meal out of the items listed above, as that information is easy to find, or just guess.

Here's a break-down of the situation:

<u>Frozen pizzas, packaged chips, cookies, and crackers, canned and bottled food, tropical fruits, pretty vegetables sealed in plastic</u> — All these things probably came 1000 miles or more. Most of them are highly-processed in a factory, with lots of chemicals added. At least half the price is for transportation, and a fuel shortage or labor strike can cut the supply at any time.

<u>Bread, dairy products, common fruits and vegetables, grains and flour</u> — These probably came from a little closer, usually 100-500 miles away. Many still require a complex factory to make them. Even simple sandwich bread is a ready-to-eat convenience food that already contain a great deal of human and machine labor, and most of the price is for that labor.

<u>Local fruits and vegetables, eggs and meat from small farms</u> — Most grocery stores won't even carry these things because the supply isn't constant. You'll have to go to a farmers' market. But if anything ever happens to our transportation system, this is all that will be for sale — not enough.

<u>Dirty turnip roots, dead chicken</u> — These are from your back yard, or the neighbor down the road. There are no processing or transportation costs, and the supply is reliable, but seasonal.

We all love pizza, Doritos, and kiwi fruits. The only question is: will you die without them?

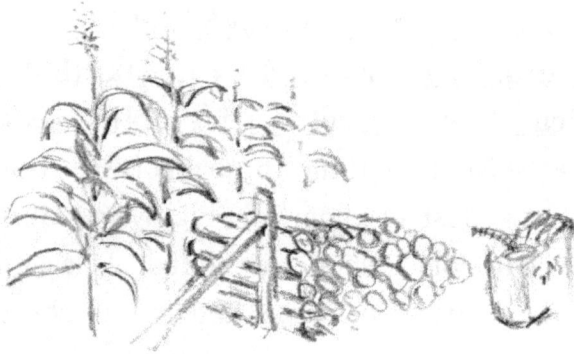

What's the Fuss?

Before the year 1700, the human population had been about 500 million (one-half billion) for a long time. That appears to be the "carrying capacity" of the planet, for people, as long as our only sources of energy were sunshine (to grow food), wind (for sailing ships and wind mills), and firewood.

Then we started using coal. In about 1900, we added crude oil (gasoline, kerosene, diesel, etc.) Finally uranium (for nuclear power) joined the party in about 1950. Those new energy sources greatly raised the "carrying capacity" of the planet, and there are now about 7 billion people in the world.

All living things reproduce as much as they can within the limits of their food supplies. If a population grows quickly, it "overshoots" the carrying capacity of the land. This damages the environment, and the population must then "die-off" to get down to the new carrying capacity, which is less than it was before the damage.

In 2005, we arrived at the "peak" of crude oil pumping, the point where we can't get more, even if the price goes way up, because of real, geological limits. Coal and uranium are harder to measure, but are doing about the same thing.

All the problems in the world, like food prices rising, unemployment, governments running out of money, and riots, are all driven by the carrying capacity ceasing to grow, and maybe starting to go down, while our population is still going up.

That was more than 300 years of human history in a nutshell. We are now in "ecological overshoot."

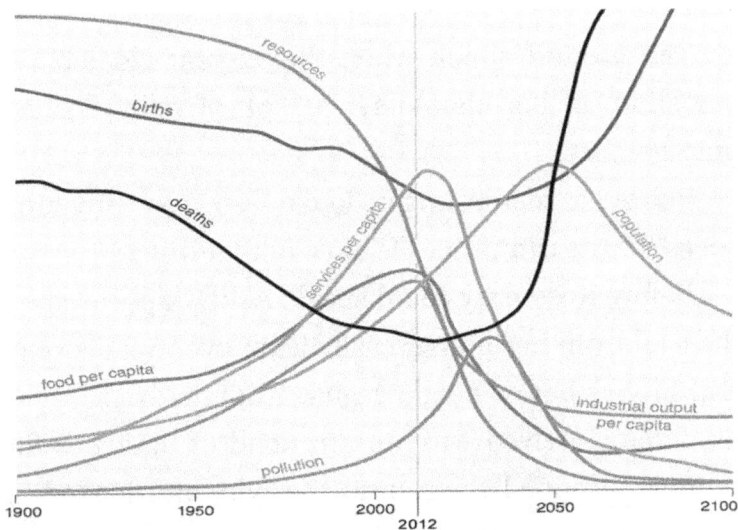

based on *The Limits to Growth*, 1972, which has matched reality very well for the last 40 years ("per capita" means per person)

Rosemary's Go-Bag

The ground shook when the 12-year-old let her bag slide off her shoulder. A look of relief flashed onto her face.

Bobby, a year younger, looked up from breaking sticks for the campfire. "What's *in* that thing?"

Before Rosemary could speak, Ashley appeared on the trail from her house, easily leapt over a fallen log, and slipped her own light go-bag from her back.

Jeremy arrived with an arm-load of branches for the fire, dropped them onto the pile, and looked at Rosemary's bulging bag. "You carried *that* all the way *here?*"

Rosemary looked defiant. "When the world ends,

I wanna have my stuff!"

Ashley sat down to help Bobby with the fire. "When, exactly, do you think the world's gonna end, Rosemary?"

The girl's defiant look softened a little as she searched her memory. "December something this year. I saw it on TV!"

The other three paid attention while Rosemary proudly brought out everything she thought she would need to survive several natural disasters, World War III, and the End of the World.

Jeremy picked up a can of pork and beans. "I bet all the water in that can — about 95% of the weight — was pretty heavy."

The 12-year-old girl cringed.

Ashley looked at Rosemary's ebook reader. "Doesn't that use the mobile phone system to load books? That's one of the first things to go in a power failure."

Rosemary looked guilty. "I thought it would save space. All my favorite books are on it."

Jeremy pointed at a small propane bottle and stove. "I've used those. They cook about 3 meals, then they're empty."

Rosemary looked sad.

"I think it's all cool," Bobby said from beside the campfire. "I'm glad I'll be your friend when the world ends. Next time you bring it, you can use my wagon."

End of the World?

Anyone who pretends to know exact dates or details about future events is lying, and probably trying to make money from it, or at least gain "followers" to make himself feel good. Although a few general trends are fairly predictable, there's no way to know exactly when they will come about, how, where, or how quickly they'll unfold.

Some things can happen quickly, like stock market crashes and riots, but even those "flash" events have roots deep in the past. Other changes are so slow it's hard to see them, like money inflation (which we'll talk about later).

The future also holds "black swan" events that cannot be predicted, like Hurricane Katrina in 2005 and the earthquake and tsunami that caused nuclear power plants in Japan to melt down in 2011.

Many "End of the World" predictions have come and gone, and those for December 2012 based on the

Mayan calendar are just as flaky as the rest.

Although a true "End of the World" is probably not coming, that doesn't mean the world isn't changing rapidly. The current economic problems (due to the rising cost of energy) can easily be traced back to about 1970. Damage to the environment from pollution, which is resulting in climate change, was well underway by 1960, with roots more than a hundred years earlier.

People have invented the phrase "The End of the World as We Know It" to describe the bumpy steps downward that appear to be what's ahead in the 21st century. These bumpy steps will probably include times when everything seems to be falling apart at once, and other times when things seem to be getting a little better.

Unfortunately, we have many ways to avoid thinking about these scary subjects. Since sex is a taboo subject, we don't like to talk about "population" problems, but instead call them something else. If a disease kills a large number of people, we talk about "sanitation" or "God's punishment," but not "carrying capacity." We find reasons to go to war, but never talk about "overshoot" and "die-off."

One thing we know for sure about human beings: we, as a species, are highly adaptable, and will most likely be able to live on the Earth as long as it will sustain life.

Rosemary's Mistake

It's impossible to put into a bag, a closet, or even a whole house, everything you'd need for the rest of your life. A year's supply of dried food, for one person, takes up a large closet, and that doesn't include water, cooking fuel, and many other things you'd need.

Rosemary's ebook reader is efficient, but not resilient (we'll talk about the difference a little later). As soon as the battery dies and she can't recharge or replace it, or the mobile phone system breaks down, the thing will be useless. Knowledge is important, but only if you can get to it when you need it.

Your go-bag is a short-term tool, meant to help with emergencies that last up to about 3 days. A strong backpacker, who carefully selects dried foods, and does not have to carry water or fuel, can pack for 3 or 4 weeks.

But for the long term, the only way to be sure you have food and other supplies is to be part of the flow of goods from gardens, farms, and workshops. In other words, it will be necessary to be part of the economic life of your community.

The image of a "survivalist" as a person who hides in a cabin deep in the woods, with stacks of canned food all around him, is not a model that would work for very long. He may have a "deeper pantry" than everyone else, but he lacks community and all its advantages: companionship, social activities, service to others, helping to raise children, cooperative projects, trade, and education, just to name a few.

Political leaders and high-level government agents will try to weather bad times by hiding in deep, hardened military bunkers. Rich people will stock vast estates with all the goods and services they're used to. Both of these are just slight variations on the "survivalist" theme, and destined to fail if the hard times last very long.

Human communities are not perfect. Like everything we do, they include both our strengths and our weaknesses. But they are sustainable and adaptable, have survived major climate changes and economic disasters in the past, and are certainly our best hope for the future.

Letting Go

Rosemary, with twelve years of accumulated wisdom to call her own, lowered her massive go-bag to the floor of her bedroom with a sigh. She carefully closed the door so no one could see, then sat down in front of her precious bag, still stuffed with everything she wanted, everything she thought she *needed* for the future.

She scrunched and moved her sore shoulders as she pulled item after item out of the bag. As pork and beans, apricots in light syrup, and creamed corn, all her favorites, went in one pile, silent tears formed in her eyes.

In another pile went her ebook reader, propane

stove and fuel bottle, stainless-steel mess kit, and one-gallon canteen. She hardly noticed the tears trickling down her cheeks.

After pulling out several more heavy things, and letting a few tears fall, she looked into her go-bag. It still contained about as much stuff as Ashley's and Jeremy's.

Her mind understood what her friends had told her. All her stuff was *great*, just not in her go-bag. But her heart wanted to be *ready*, wherever she was, any time of the day or night.

After a deep breath and a sigh, Rosemary picked up her go-bag with it's remaining contents: a few Power Bars, a little first-aid kit, and the other things all her friends had. It felt *wonderful* compared to the last time she had lifted it. She almost wanted to put it on and take a walk.

A resolute expression formed on her face. Maybe she would take a walk later, but right now, after wiping her face on her sleeves, she wanted to clear off a shelf in her closet. If she couldn't keep pork and beans, apricots in light syrup, and creamed corn with her all the time, they would at least have a place of honor in her ... in her deep pantry!

As Rosemary worked, she realized how lucky she was to have friends who would be honest with her. It would be much harder, she realized, to prepare for the future without them.

A Strange Enemy

As the "carrying capacity" of the planet drops below what we'd like (plenty to eat and a good life for everyone), we put on our thinking caps and come up with "solutions." Most of them involve doing more with less, in other words, "efficiency."

Who could possibly complain about efficiency? It gives us more of the good things of life at less cost. It "solves" our problems. Or does it?

Electric heat, the most efficient kind, is a good example. If you only count the electricity that comes into your house, and the heat it makes, it's 100% efficient! Very few things can make that claim.

But then problems start popping up. To be 100% efficient, we have to keep the windows closed. The air gets stale (low oxygen), humid (high moisture), and full of germs, chemicals, and odors.

If we were machines, efficiency alone might work for us. But we are flesh-and-blood creatures who have many needs and desires, and one of them is to have babies. As soon as we free up resources through efficiency, people feel comfortable enough to have more children (or children live who would have died in a poorer world), the population rises, and the additional people soak up the extra resources.

And it gets worse.

Efficiency not only fails to help us live within the carrying capacity of the planet, it creates traps for us. When things are most efficient, they are light, thin, and break easily. On the other hand, when things are durable, robust, and "resilient," they are usually not very efficient.

Returning to our beloved electric heat: a tree falls on the wires 25 miles away, and soon our houses grow cold. Our highly-efficient electric heat has failed completely.

"Resilience" is the ability to experience changes and take shocks without breaking. Changes and shocks are becoming more and more common. Because of that, many of our "efficient" machines and systems will no longer serve us well.

The *least* efficient heating fuel is wood, but as long as you have a winter's worth all cut, chopped, and dry, you have a highly-resilient source of heat that almost no external event can touch.

The most resilient of all heating systems, and much more portable than firewood, is necessary wherever you go in the winter — a good warm coat.

Essential First-Aid

Just 5 **B**'s to remember, in this order ...

<u>Heart**B**eat?</u> Yes, yours is beating. What about your little brother who just got an electric shock? He's got about one minute to live. Cardio-pulmonary resuscitation (CPR) involves working the heart and lungs as much as possible from outside the body until they (hopefully) get the message and start working on their own again. You have to get training for this, but it's easy to find and just takes a few hours. If you're not trained to do this, then you're not serious about preparing for a future with family and friends at your side.

<u>**B**reath?</u> Of course there's always air to breathe, unless your sister is choking on a piece of food, is drowning, or the air's full of smoke. The food or

water has to be forced out with deep compressions of the abdomen and diaphragm (you'll learn this in any First-Aid class). You must get yourself and others *out* of smoke quickly. It may not go all the way down to the floor, so crawling might be the only way to go.

<u>**B**leeding?</u>   Real, live, red stuff gushing out of a deep cut. You have to stop it NOW. No, you can't super-glue or duct tape it, and you probably can't even use a First-Aid kit, as most don't have enough compresses. That's right, you'll probably have to use your hands, which means you'll have to touch the blood, and probably get it all over you. Either do it, or wave good-bye.

Once the bleeding has slowed down, cloth may help. Use the cleanest you have. Eventually, the wound can be closed, the area cleaned, and the wound dressed. Learn more in a First-Aid class.

<u>**B**roken **B**ones?</u> Now you can slow down a little. The important thing is to keep the person still, or at least the part of the body with the broken bone. If the bone has broken the skin, that's a bleeding problem. If the person is in so much pain they go unconscious, watch the heart**B**eat and **B**reathing closely.

<u>**B**urns?</u>   1st degree burns are just red and need little care. 2nd degree are blistered — keep them clean and unbroken. 3rd degree burns crack or char the skin, must be kept clean (plastic wrap or bag), and the person will need antibiotics.

First-Aid Class

Jeremy knew everyone was looking at him, but he remained silent until he had the campfire going well. The looks on their faces begged him to reassure them that they, too, would survive the ordeal.

Finally he cleared his throat. "Well ... it was kinda weird at first. *Everyone* was way older than me, and everyone was doing it because they *had* to for their job or something. But I said to myself, "Self ..."

His friends laughed, and he smiled back at them.

"... it doesn't matter why *other* people are here, *I'm* here to learn this stuff so I can save my family and friends' lives if I ever need to."

He could see Ashley nodding.

"They spent lots of time telling us all the things we *shouldn't* do, you know, because only doctors and nurses did that stuff. I kept my mouth shut. Finally we got to the stuff we *were* supposed to learn, and they had a plastic dummy we could practice CPR on."

"But what about ... germs?" Rosemary asked with a twisted face.

"They used alcohol pads on the dummy's mouth between each person."

The girl looked relieved.

"But the biggest thing, after CPR, was bleeding. We got to practice on each other. The teacher drew cuts on us with red felt pens, and we had to stop the pretend-bleeding, then bandage it."

Bobby's eyes were round. Rosemary squirmed.

"She showed us how, for different parts of the body," Jeremy continued, "then *we* had to do it. Once, the teacher kept saying, 'It hasn't stopped,' then finally, 'He just bled out and died.' The guy with the big felt-pen gash gave a little speech, then pretended to croak. I think he was a drama teacher or something."

Ashley chuckled. Rosemary thought about it, then smiled.

"There was some splinting — you know, little ones for fingers, big ones for arms and legs — and some burn wrapping. Carrying an injured person, a few other things. Nothing we can't handle."

Ashley, Bobby, and Rosemary looked at each other with unsure faces for a long moment, but eventually cracked tiny smiles.

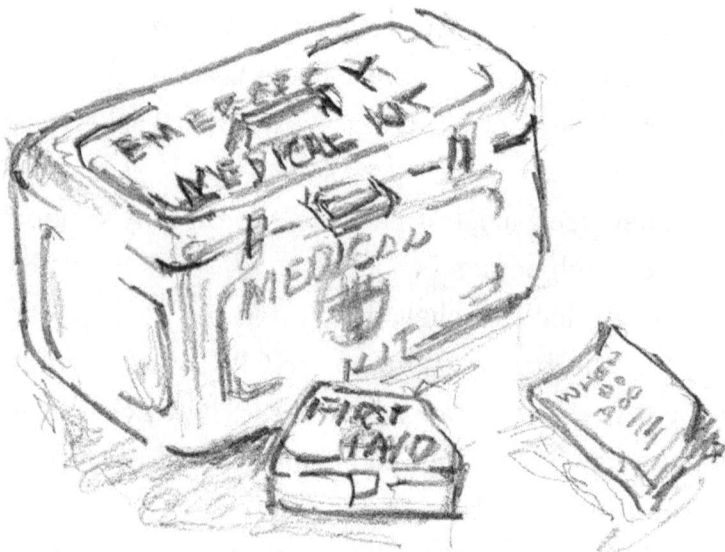

Beyond First-Aid

"First-Aid" is designed around the assumption that an ambulance is on the way, and a hospital is not far. Because of that, First-Aid classes and books tell you many things you should *not* do. They have to do that, as our legal system would treat anyone as a criminal who did more without being a medic, nurse, or medical doctor.

But if that ambulance and hospital are not available, you may have to go beyond First-Aid and do your best to accomplish the things doctors would do. The law allows this, as long as you have good reasons to believe that professional medical care is not available (at least, in time).

In the coming years, you may have to deal with

medical problems when the medical system is *completely* unable to respond, at all, ever. It may be overwhelmed by large numbers of patients, inaccessible because of transportation problems, squeezed by budget cuts, or simply unwilling to help people without insurance or large sums of money.

Whatever the cause, you may find yourself needing much more than a First-Aid kit. A robust family medical kit, capable of dealing with many problems a First-Aid kit cannot, should be part of every household that plans to survive the unpredictable future. It should be kept in a large, clean tool box so it can be easily moved, instead of the pieces scattered among several cabinets and drawers. Most medical supplies are freely available "over the counter" or on the internet.

The primary exception is prescription drugs. If the medical system ceases to work, they will become unavailable to most people. Fortunately, some of the most important ones (such as broad-spectrum antibiotics like tetracycline, "Terramycin," and penicillin) are available from livestock supply houses for animals.

You should also get copies of the books *Where There Is No Doctor*, by David Werner, and *Where There is No Dentist*, by Murray Dickson, which may be downloaded for free from many places on the internet, including www.nebador.com/TwoFeet.html.

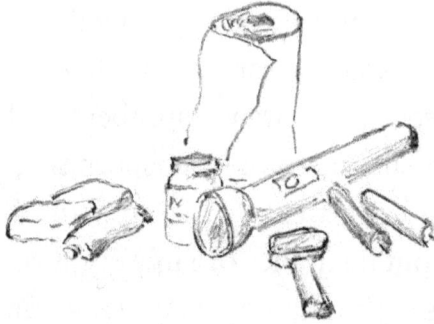

Drugs and Blades!

"What would be in this ... what did you call it ... medical kit?" Bobby's mother asked, most of her mind on the casserole she was making.

Bobby, at the kitchen table, sparkled with hope. "I have a list! It's all the stuff that little First-Aid kits can't do."

She glanced down while beating eggs in a bowl. "Looks like drugs and such! There's no way ..."

"Mom! Musenex is an expectorant, it clears your throat and lungs! Benadryl is an antihistamine for allergies! Imodium is diarrhea medicine!"

"What's this? Scalpel blades? I've heard about teenagers cutting themselves ..."

"What are you gonna do if I get a deep, infected splinter?"

"Take you to the doctor, of course!"

Just then Bobby's father wandered in from the living room with a wrinkled brow. "I'll take a look at it, honey. How long until dinner?"

Here are most of the things you'd find in a good robust family medical kit:

Flashlight, white glow sticks, candle, matches
Medical shears, pocket knife
Gauze pads, gauze rolls, feminine hygiene pads
Paper towels, cloth towels, sheet material
Tape, "Band-Aids" (large), butterfly bandages
Safety pins, nylon cord, splint/tongue sticks
Elastic "Ace" bandages
Needles, tweezers, scalpels, magnifying glass
Thermometers (glass, electronic w/covers)
Providone iodine, hydrogen peroxide, hand sanitizer,
    70% isopropyl alcohol: antiseptics
Water, apple cider vinegar, saline solution
Petroleum jelly, water-based lubricating jelly
Aspirin, ibuprofen, "Tylenol": analgesics
"Benadryl" antihistamine, "Imodium" antidiarrheal
"Musenex" expectorant and cough suppressant
Ipecac syrup: emetic, expectorant
Eucalyptus/menthol cough drops, hard candy
Hydrocortisone cream antipruritic
"Triple Antibiotic" ointment
"Tums," sodium bicarbonate, activated charcoal
Eye cup, otoscope, blood pressure cuff
Dental picks, dental emergency kit
Burn gel, plastic burn wrap
Hot packs, cold packs, felt bunion pads

Your Parents?

It would be great if your parents were on your team in some way, as they can usually bring extra knowledge and resources to your preparations. Most parents know more about stocking a pantry, and tending minor medical problems, than you will know even after reading several books and taking several classes.

But having your parents on your team would require some special conditions.

First of all, there must be a good level of mutual respect between you and them. Standing on your own two feet is basically a "grown up" thing. If your parents are not ready to see and accept that part of you, then you will probably not be able to think of them as team members.

Next, you have to see if they're "in denial." Many people will be clinging to the hope that by going on with "business as usual" (in other words, *not* preparing for anything), somehow everything will be okay. They may react with hostility or ridicule toward anyone who has a different approach, like maybe you.

Finally, do they have any time or resources to contribute? Many parents will be working as hard as they can just to pay the rent and put a little food on the table. But even then, they may be able to answer your questions, about things they know, if you ask nicely when they're relaxed and have a little free time.

These and other issues will determine if your parents can be on your team, if they can just contribute some resources to your effort, or if you and your friends are completely on your own.

Please be gentle with them. They are, after all, only human. In most cases, they followed society's rules. They went into debt for a mortgage on a house, just like everyone else. They got jobs that would only exist while energy was cheap and plentiful, just like everyone else. They stocked only shallow pantries, just like everyone else.

Most young adults, probably including you, would do the exact same thing if you had the chance. But considering the forces at work in the world, it doesn't look like you'll get that chance.

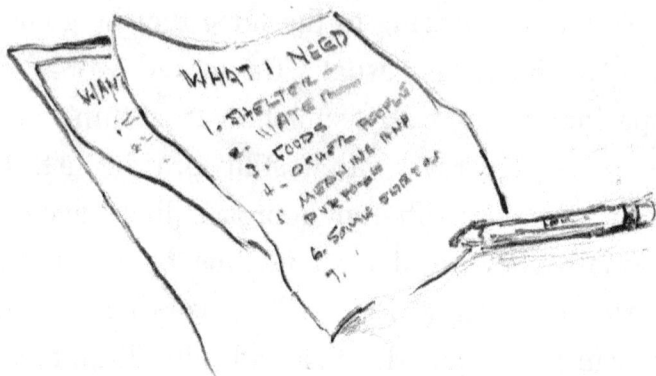

What do we NEED?

People can't live in a "vacuum." We are biological beings, animals, mammals, who must have connections to our world on many levels.

Our connections start with Planet Earth. Without air pressure close to one "atmosphere," which is 20% or so oxygen, we will die in minutes. Temperatures outside of about 10-40°C (50-100°F) will kill us in a few hours without protective clothing.

Without a quart (liter) of water a day, we won't last a week. If we can't scrape up a thousand calories of food every day, we'll waste away in a month or less. Protein, vitamins, and minerals are also necessary, or diseases will get us.

Beyond the basics, we need safety from whatever

dangers are lurking about, and shelter from sun, wind, rain, and snow.

If we have all that, we might be alive, but we won't be happy.

We are social creatures who need companionship and love. We are dependent on parents for five years in a simple society, and ten, fifteen, maybe even twenty years in a complex society. We need friends to share thoughts and experiences. Most of us need a lover, and someday a mate and children.

Some of us are happy with that much. Some of us aren't.

We need meaning and purpose. Skills and abilities, and a job or business in which to use them, bring that for many people. Some need an art medium with which to express their creativity. Some need sources of knowledge and learning. A few crave to exercise power.

What do *you* need? There are probably clues all over your bedroom. Pictures and posters on your walls, or books on your shelves, probably say a lot about what you want to do as a profession in the future, and what kinds of people you want to have relationships with.

It's okay if some of those dreams aren't realistic right now. Your interactions with the real world, when you set out to make your dreams come true, will bring them into line with reality very quickly.

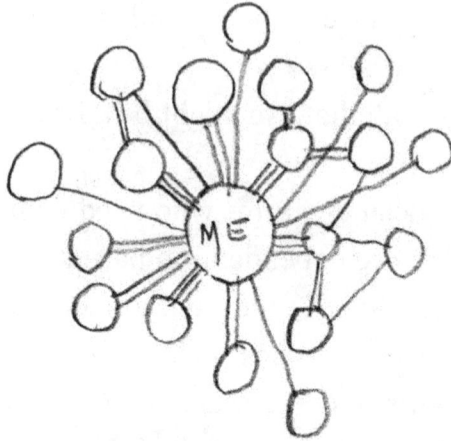

Your Web of Life

Get blank paper, pencil, and eraser. Write "ME" in the middle, and close around that, put the things and people most essential to you. A little farther away, put the things and people that are important but not essential. Farther away still, those that are nice but not too important ... you get the idea. Maybe farthest away would go those things and people you need and have to put up with, but don't really like, such as a grumpy boss if you have a job.

Draw different kinds of lines from "ME" to each thing or person, perhaps a single line to friends, a double line to your boy/girlfriend, a dotted line to someone you just have to put up with, or whatever seems right to you. Some of the other people on your diagram have relationships between them, such as your parents, who were mates, or your friends, who might also be friends with each other.

Don't be surprised if you have to re-draw your Web of Life several times to get it right. Also, it will change from year to year, maybe more often, and need to be redone. That's natural.

It's a powerful tool for understanding what you *need* to be happy, what's important to you, and what's not so important. By looking at it, you might get ideas for things you want to change. Some of us have cravings or addictions we want to get rid of. Others are lonely and have a place in our lives for a friend or boy/girlfriend. Maybe there are classes you have your eye on, things you want to learn in order to pursue your life goals.

If you have a good level of trust with your team, you might want to share your Web of Life with them. If that level of trust doesn't yet exist, maybe sharing your Web of Life will help it to grow.

Another use of the Web of Life is to draw one as your life is now, and another as you *want* your life to be in 5 or 10 years. By comparing the two, you can get a pretty good idea of what you need to do to move toward your goals.

But remember to give some thought to which of your goals can be followed by sheer force of will (with tools and information that are easy to get), and which might be blocked by a bad economy, civil unrest, or other problems in the world.

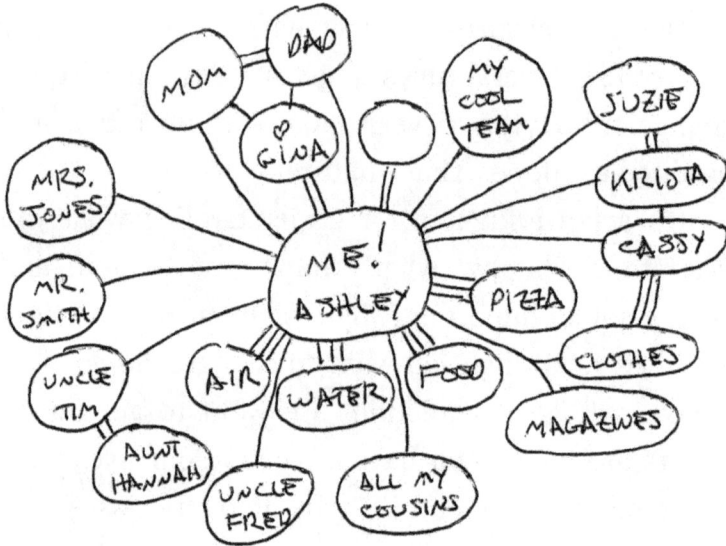

Ashley's Web

"I've been *called* a spider before, but this is the first time I had to spin my own web!"

Bobby, who had already shared his Web of Life, laughed deeply. Jeremy, who knew he was next, smiled but looked a little nervous.

"Closest to me, as you know, is my little sister. But I drew an empty circle for a cute boy someday ..."

Rosemary grinned.

"Air, water, and food, all that stuff, are close too. Then come my parents and you guys. I was a little surprised to discover that my ... you know ... my fair-weather friends at school were further away. I guess that's because I don't think many of them are gonna make it when life gets rough. They *need* the mall. They haven't noticed that it's half-empty, and getting worse."

"The mall's really good at disguising the empty spaces," Jeremy said.

Ashley nodded. "Then I have a couple of uncles, an aunt, and some cousins I don't see very often. They're all okay, but nothing special. In the same row, I put one of my teachers, and Mrs. Jones, that cool librarian."

"What about Fang?" Rosemary asked with concern.

"Oops! He's gonna slobber all over me for forgetting him. Let me see ... honestly ... here with my parents and team."

"We're really ... just as important as your ... parents?" Jeremy asked timidly.

"Yeah!" Ashley asserted. "This isn't some fantasy adventure game, you know. *You* guys are gonna be there, at my side, when the sh ... poop hits the fan. My parents are too, although they're still half in-denial. They'll grow out of it. I'm working on them, with the help of news articles I accidentally on-purpose leave open on the internet."

Bobby flopped backwards and rolled on the ground with laughter. Jeremy and Rosemary managed to stay on their logs, but barely.

Happiness

It's not something you find, get, or buy. It has nothing to do with how much money you have. It's something you choose.

If you and I each have a can of beans, we have two choices. We can sit in our corners, eat our own beans quickly, and glance up often to make sure the other person isn't planning to steal our beans.

Or, I can give my can of beans to you. No, I'm not looking at your can of beans (thinking it's better), I'm just sitting and smiling. And I just offered you a relationship.

You think about it for a minute, then give me your can of beans. You just accepted the relationship. We both smile.

We both now have the same amount of food we started with. But we are both much happier, and the relationship we just began might be worth much more than beans, much more than even gold.

There are powerful forces in the world that would like us to think we need money, a job, a house (and a mortgage, of course), health insurance, a bank account, a good credit rating, a telephone — you know the list — in order to be happy. We certainly *can* be happy if we happen to have those things. The question is, what are you going to do if you *don't* have those things?

"Count your blessings." It's an old saying. Recall for a moment what you are *guaranteed* when you are born. Some people say, "Death and taxes." You might, in some cases, be able to avoid the taxes. What does that leave?

For about 99% of the history of the human race, our ancestors were what we call "cave men." (Yes, they're back there somewhere on our family trees.) A typical cave man or woman could claim these possessions, if they were lucky:
— an animal skin for a blanket
— a crude knife made from a sharp rock
— a spear made from a slender tree
— a water bottle made from a gourd
That's about it. What do *you* have? Are you happy?

Get Real

As you probably know, most of your adult citizenship rights and responsibilities, in most places, kick in when you turn 18. There are places where you might also gain certain adult rights at 9, 13, 14, 16, 17, 19, 20, 21, or 24. The details won't fit in this book, so you should find out what ages give you what rights in your location: voting, signing contracts, banking, marriage, driving, working, smoking, drinking, military service ...

In the USA, young people under 18 can do many things, especially if you are willing and able to act fairly grown-up.

There are 3 things you can get that will help you do business in the world. All 3 cost some money, so be prepared.

The first is your **birth certificate**. If you think, or are told, that your parents have it somewhere safe so you can't have it, that's not true. Your parents have a "certified copy" of your birth certificate. No one has the original, except the government agency that keeps them. There can be many certified copies. Some states require you to already have a photo ID, so you might need your parent's help getting your birth certificate, or the photo ID (next item).

A **state ID card** works as identification just like a driver's license, and is usually issued by the same government agency, but is for non-drivers and minors. You'll probably need a parent and your birth certificate to get yours.

Lots of things require 2 pieces of ID, and a "student ID card" is rarely accepted. The best one to get next is a **passport**. Parent, birth certificate, state ID card, and two photos (to their specs) should do the trick. Sometimes, like if your birth certificate was "delayed," they require more stuff, so it's good to get this done long before you want to travel anywhere. A passport is good as ID even after it expires.

One reason to get these things now is that they probably require a little help from a parent. During troubled times, parents and kids sometimes get separated. If you're ready with these 3 items, you'll be much more prepared for whatever the future brings.

Buying Stuff

Minors in the USA can buy most things* with cash, and also can buy and use postal money orders, allowing you to make mail-order purchases from many businesses. (Any business that says it will take "checks" will also take money orders.)

The key to successfully doing business in the world is to act, speak, and write like an adult. If your business is legal, there's no reason to make your age an issue. Most businesses don't *care* how old you are. As long as your money is good, they're happy.

But if you reveal your age, they might get nervous, and start *wondering* if maybe there's some law they don't know about, and then say "no" just to be safe.

For example, if you *ask* the postal clerk if you can

buy a money order, you're inviting them to find some reason to be prejudiced against you. An adult just steps up to the counter and says, "I need a money order for twenty dollars and ..."

Anything that is actually forbidden to minors will say so right on the web site or in the catalog.

But if you can't keep yourself and your friends from "goofing off" in person, if your telephone voice is sprinkled with giggles and oh-my-gods, and if your handwriting looks like crayon, you may have trouble buying even so much as a lollipop.

If you know what you want, model number, price, etc., and realize there will be taxes and shipping charges added, you can probably get your questions answered on the telephone or by email. Then, with good handwriting and a postal money order, you can probably buy anything* you want.

By the way, "handwriting" does not need to be cursive script. Manuscript (printing) is just fine, and probably even better for most things. The only exception is your signature. It should be flowing cursive script, but does not have to be readable, and a hard-to-copy flair is even a good idea. It should, however, look about the same every time you do it.

✳

* Except tobacco, alcohol, firearms, a few other controlled substances, X-rated stuff, and things that require contracts (like telephone service).

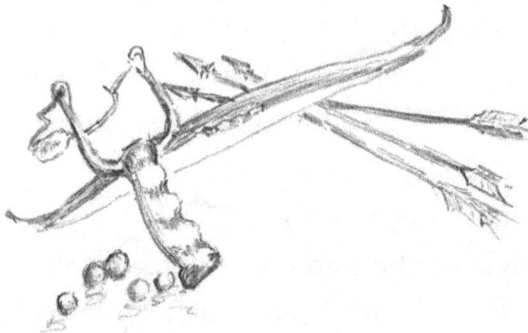

Jeremy's "Firearm"

"This is totally out of my comfort zone," he said as he lined up 3 pop cans on a log about a hundred feet from the campfire. "That's why I kept it a secret from *everyone* until I wasn't a complete klutz at it."

Bobby chuckled under his breath. Jeremy flashed him a warning glance.

"As you guys know, I'm much more comfortable with words and numbers ..."

"We know," Ashley said. "That why you get to help me with my homework about 3 times a week!"

Jeremy grinned sheepishly. "I couldn't get the best price, because some places don't take checks or money orders anymore. But I found one, they have a huge sporting goods catalog, and I'm gonna get more stuff from them, stuff you can't get here in town."

Ashley and the others watched intently as Jeremy pulled a weird metal, plastic, and rubber thing from a leather case, twisted the handle around, and it became a serious-looking slingshot.

"It was scary buying a money order for the first time. I was afraid my body language would scream *little kid feeling guilty*. I don't think I breathed the whole time I was in the post office, but nothing happened."

As the others watched, Jeremy tapped the bottom of the handle, a marble slid out, he skillfully slipped it into the leather pouch, pulled, and a second later one of the pop cans burst into the air and disappeared somewhere behind the log.

Rosemary and Bobby both jumped.

"It won't stop a bear or bring down an elk, but I hope that I'll get good enough to bring home a rabbit someday."

"We've got lots of them in our bushes!" Bobby said, eyeing the powerful slingshot.

"Poor bunnies ..." Rosemary moaned.

※

As you can see, not all "firearms" are forbidden to minors (although slingshots are illegal in a very few places because some gangs use them). Archery equipment and traps are also available. Some basic hunting or trapping skills might be valuable for young adults who live in places with game animals. The drawback is that large game will quickly be cleaned out by adults with rifles during bad times. The supply of rabbits, birds, and other small animals will be much more sustainable.

Emotional Resilience

One of the most powerful tools for dealing with a changing world is the ability to keep our heads (minds) in control, even when our hearts (emotions) would rather be.   This is also called Emotional Intelligence, but there's an even older and simpler term: "maturity."   If your emotions are always in control, you're a child, no matter how old you are.

This does not mean *not* feeling. Our emotions are very important when we need to sense things about our environment, make judgments about people and situations, and form bonds (or reject them).

What it does mean is *feeling* the feelings, not *acting* on them. That's the key. If you feel something and act on it without thought, you're a slave to your emotions. Slaves are seldom treated well by other people or events in the world.

But if you *feel* the feelings, then *decide* what to do with a clear head, you have the best chance of staying alive and being happy.

Yeah, I know. Easier said than done.

Once you clearly understand the idea of keeping

your mind in control even when feeling, and decide you want to do that, the next step is to practice. You can't really practice at times and places you choose, but instead you just have to wait for emotional situations to pop up in life, do your best, and look back to see how you did after it's over.

Here are some suggestions that might help:

Never do anything dangerous, if it can be avoided, when feeling deeply, even if you think your mind is in control. If nothing else, your reaction time will be slowed. Good pilots never fly aircraft when feeling emotional. Remember: driving is a kind of piloting.

Never make big, important decisions, if they can be avoided, when feeling deeply. Your rational mind, even if in control, is not operating on "all cylinders." Save decisions about education, employment, marriage, etc., for when you are clear-headed.

If everything is basically okay in your world right now (parent has a job, food in the cupboards), it may be hard to see how important this stuff is. But the world is changing rapidly, and many young adults may soon find themselves dealing with difficult, sometimes dangerous situations. You might have a parent, friend, or boy/girlfriend at your side to help, or you might be alone. Even if someone is with you, you might discover that *they* are consumed with emotions, and *you* will have to think clearly, if anyone is going to.

Bobby Coming of Age

"Somehow ... that sounds familiar ..." Bobby said, almost to himself as he gazed into the flames of the campfire.

"You have a story to share?" Ashley asked.

The boy was silent for a long moment. "It ... wasn't that long ago. When I was ... about 8. I used to ... this is hard to say ... I used to yell and scream when I didn't get my way."

Everyone could sense how hard this was for Bobby, so no one said anything until Ashley finally spoke. "We don't care what you were like at 8, only what you're like now."

Bobby cracked a slight smile and took a deep

breath. "I was a brat. I couldn't say it then, but lots of other people did. Then one day, after yelling at me and spanking me so hard I cried, my dad asked me ... you know, after we both settled down ... he asked me, 'Is this the kind of person you want to be?' I didn't say anything, but I knew, in my heart, that the answer was *no*."

"Wow," Rosemary breathed.

"Somehow ... that spanking ... and that question ... did something to change me. I think ... I grew up more that day than ... years before that. I couldn't ... you know ... be on this team now if that hadn't happened."

Jeremy nodded.

"After that, there was a little part of me that could still think, even when I was mad as hell, or afraid, or anything. And that little part gave me something to hold onto while I let the feelings go and, you know, chilled out."

Ashley grinned.

"I still feel lots of stuff, but I know now it's not really me, it's just something I'm feeling, you know, for a little while."

Everyone was silent for a few minutes as they pondered Bobby's experience.

Eventually a soft voice was heard. "Sometimes ... I need to ... learn that a little better ... too."

Bobby, Rosemary, and Jeremy all nodded.

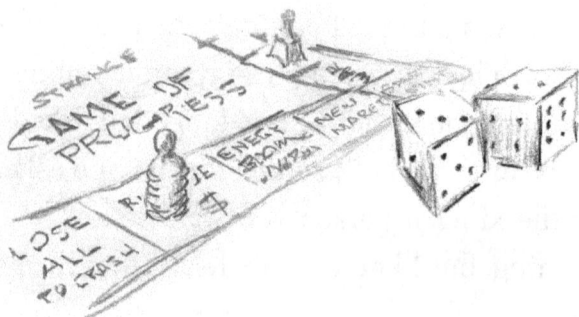

Our Myths

When we were young, we all learned a number of stories about how the universe works. They were designed to fill gaps in our actual human knowledge, because we just *hate* not knowing things. Here are a few you need to know about in order to clearly see what's happening in the world:

Everything will constantly be getting bigger, better, faster, richer, and children will always have more than their parents had! This is called the "Myth of Progress," and was invented to describe the period of cheap and abundant energy that started about 1700 and appears to have peaked in 2005. Although we like to think our civilization will always be spiraling upward toward a glorious future, it doesn't fit with the reality that we live on a planet with clear limits, and that no other habitable planets are available.

The future will be about like the past! It's natural to assume tomorrow will be about like today.

In reality, tomorrow can be very different. The USA and Europe have been unusually stable during the last 2/3 of a century. Most of human history has been much more turbulent and unpredictable.

Technology will save us! When people have stuff to work with (energy, minerals, etc.), they get creative and invent all kinds of things. But it won't happen if the necessary stuff is too expensive or non-existent.

We can, and must, keep growing our population and economy forever! Maybe we think we must, but we cannot. Infinite growth of any kind is impossible in a finite (limited) environment. The Earth is just a ball, with a thin film of life on the surface.

Global trade will make everyone rich! The globalization of our economy, which began in the 1950s and went into high gear in the 1980s, has improved the lives of many people, but has also caused the greatest concentration of wealth, in the hands of the fewest people, since just before the Great Depression (1930s). It has also created a very fragile "just in time" world distribution system. Today, global trade appears to be winding down.

We're exceptional! It can't happen to us! This time is different! It doesn't matter who says this, it's immature and ignores everything we've ever learned from all the sciences and all of history.

Black or White?

One more myth, so important it deserves its own chapter, because there are many powerful forces in the world who try to control us with this myth, usually quite successfully.

"If you're not with us, you're against us!"

"America, Love It or Leave It!"

"Liberal or Conservative!"

"Christ or The Devil!"

"Science or Religion!"

It's used in a thousand more ways, all of them designed to force us to make an extreme choice, when in reality we only had a slight preference, or none at all. We then feel we must accept *all* the things about the side we chose that we *don't* like.

For thousands of years, this has been recognized as a *logical fallacy*, an error in thinking, a way the human mind tends to miss reality. It's call *False Dilemma*, and comes in 2 flavors:

A or B?   C!   The possibilities are presented as

exhaustive, but in reality there are other options.

A, B, or C? Some A, lots of B, and a bit of C! The possibilities are presented as *mutually exclusive*, but in reality a combination is possible.

If you learn to spot this fallacy, you will find it *everywhere* in the news and in opinions that people express. It has only one purpose — to take away your freedom of thought. True, some people like being told what to think. In a sense, it makes life easier. What it *doesn't* do is get you prepared for hard times.

There are many logical fallacies and other kinds of thinking errors, too many to fit in this book. If you want to learn more about them, any good book on "critical thinking" will help, and a page on the author's web site has a long list of them, with explanations and examples. Here are a few:

Ad Populum — Lots of people believe it, so it must be true!

Post Hoc — This came before that, so it must be the cause of that!

Sour Grapes — If I can't get it, it must not be any good!

Naturalistic Fallacy — It's common, so it must be good!

Disdainful Dismissal — Your idea is ... just a bunch of pooh-pooh!

Genetic Fallacy — That weirdo thought of it, so it must be wrong!

Money Without Jobs

People have been making money without "real" jobs ever since there was money. In fact, "real" jobs have been very rare until the 20th century.

But now, it looks like young adults are going to again find a world with few "real" jobs when they get out of high school or college. Some of you will get lucky, and some will be helped by family connections. But many young people, it appears, will have great trouble competing for the few remaining jobs. Every person's situation is different, but maybe one of these ideas will be just right for you:

Casual labor — Young adults have a long history of doing little jobs for people that would not make sense to hire an adult to do, even part-time. Yard work, painting, recycling, house cleaning ... the list goes on. Elderly people especially need these services, an hour here, two hours there.

Value adding — We have become such a

throw-away culture that we've forgotten how useful things can be if given a little fixing up. Perhaps you've seen grandma scraping out a peanut butter jar, washing it, filling it with something beautiful (but inexpensive, like colored macaroni), and making a gift out of it. We call this the "depression mentality." Well, guess what! It may be just the mentality you will need to live and prosper in the future.

Bartering — Who needs money? It makes trading more flexible, but if you don't have any, you don't have any. What *do* you have? Someone who has something you want will probably be much more willing to part with it if you offer something in exchange, even if it's not something they really need. They might know someone who can use it, even if they cannot.

Community — When economic times are bad, one of the greatest assets you can have is a community that knows you. When you can't find a job, no one has money for casual labor, you can't find anything to fix up, and you have nothing to barter with, just give of your time and skills. If you start doing things for people that they are unable to do (as with elderly people), or don't have time to do (as with people who have jobs), they will, with rare exceptions, make sure you are compensated. Maybe all they can do is make you a simple meal. If you're hungry, maybe that's all you need.

Ashley's Job

Ashley was scared.

What she was about to do went against everything she had been taught. To get a job, except a little yard work, you had to graduate high school, maybe even college. You had to put in applications, and have interviews. When you were hired, you were given a number, an ID card, and at least a few hours of orientation and training.

She stepped over boxes and bags of junk on the old wooden porch, trying to get to the creepy front door, but it wasn't easy. Three cats eyed her from nooks and perches, one licking its paws. Something smelled bad, as if another cat, somewhere on the cluttered porch, had met its fate a while back.

When you got a job, Ashley had always believed, you got paid in money, or with a check you could take to the bank. Now she had read in 3 different places that if you really wanted to work, and be a part of your community, you just had to start, money or no. And Jeremy said it worked.

But the doorbell *didn't* work, so Ashley knocked. After a long wait, the door creaked open. An ancient lady peered through tri-focal glasses. "Yes, little girl?"

Ashley, at fifteen years of age, was tempted to correct the old lady, then remembered that to someone that old, *everyone* seemed like a child.

"Hi ... um ... I'm Ashley, I live just down the road, and ... um ... I'd like to work for you, do anything you need done ..."

"But honey, I don't have any money. My son pays the bills and has groceries delivered."

Ashley wrestled, for a long moment, with her burning desire to somehow earn some money. She could hear part of her mind saying, *I need at least $5 an hour*.

"That's okay," Ashley replied with her heart in her throat. "I don't need any money."

"Well, let me think," the elderly lady began, glancing behind her. "I don't suppose I've done the dishes in about a week, and I never seem to find time for the cat boxes ..."

Community

As we've talked about before, almost no one can survive hard times alone. Young adults will need all the help they can get from parents, team, and community.

Your parents are stuck with you, your team truly knows you as a person, but your community usually goes by reputation. Whether you call it "social networking" or "gossip," people tell each other their experiences. Their experiences with you will decide if they have work for you to do, or an extra plate of food, during hard times.

You can establish a good reputation as an individual, but doing it as a team might be even more useful. Your team could bring a wider variety of skills and tools to any task. Your team can keep working even if one member (like maybe *you*) is sick on a day you've promised to do something.

This method of being a respected member of your community was used by Saint Francis of Assisi, but he certainly didn't invent it. Here's the reputation you, or your team, needs to build to get ready for hard times:

Flexible — You'll do whatever you're able, are willing to learn new things quickly, and aren't afraid to get your hands dirty.

Humble — You aren't concerned with pay, and will be glad for whatever you get. Some people may not have money, but will feed you, or give you stuff from their gardens. If you truly feel cheated by someone, you can avoid working for them again. *They* will get a reputation, the bad kind.

Honorable — You finish what you start, and fix any mistakes you make, even if you must put in extra time without pay.

Trustworthy — You never touch anything that isn't part of the assigned task, or in any other way violate the trust of working in someone's home or on their land.

If your team builds this kind of reputation *before* you need it, you will probably find people asking for your services at a time when few people, even adults, can find work of any kind. Remember, you're not trying to get rich. With rare exceptions, that's no longer possible. You're trying to survive and be happy.

Ashley's Pay

Ashley got comfortable at the campfire circle and grinned with pride as she pulled an old crumpled paper sack from her go-bag.

"Did you go dumpster-diving?" Jeremy asked, pulling up his hood against a light mist.

"No! I got a job. You wouldn't *believe* the messes that need cleaning up in Mrs. White's old house. I must have swamped out *five* cat boxes. They were so bad, the cats refused to go near them."

Bobby laughed deeply. "I thought that place was haunted!"

"No, just really old, and kind of ... dark. She paid me so much, I'm going to buy her some new light bulbs."

"Paid?" Jeremy questioned, eyes wide.

Ashley emptied the contents of the crumpled sack onto her go-bag. "An old $2 bill, $4.57 in change *plus* a silver quarter, and a pair of earrings she hasn't worn in ages but she thought they'd look good on me. Oh yeah, a tuna sandwich and an apple."

Rosemary picked up an earring. "Could those be ... diamonds?"

Ashley grinned. "Maybe. I'm gonna ask at the jewelry store tomorrow, then tell Mrs. White what they're worth. And I'm going back on Saturday to start on her refrigerator ... *after* doing the cat boxes, of course."

Rosemary scrunched her face and pinched her nose.

＊

Elderly people have often collected things of value they no longer need or want. They sometimes need help with everyday chores, repair work, and even personal care, and might be happy to pass a few of their possessions along when they find a young adult who treats them with kindness and respect. That includes being honest if the value of something turns out to be unexpectedly high.

This kind of work is usually fairly easy, but you must be prepared to accept the inflexibility that comes with age. An elderly person may want things done a certain way. Consider it practice for a "real" job, as many employers are just as inflexible.

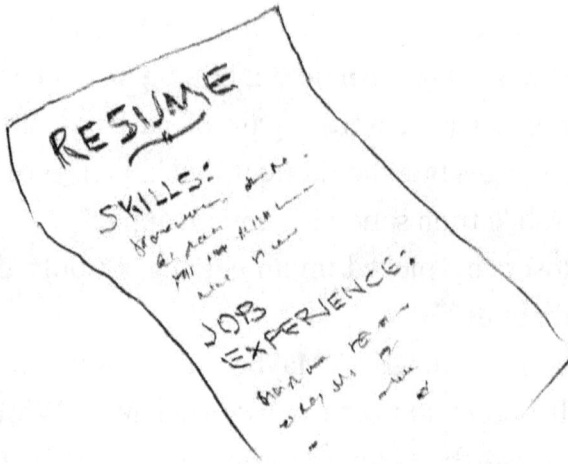

Your Skills

Don't have any? That's okay. You'll gain them quickly *if* you have a good attitude.

Good attitude? See the list of values you need for a good community reputation, a couple of chapters back.

If you get out there and start doing things for people, they'll usually explain what you need to know, sometimes work with you for a while. But they'll expect you to *get it* the first or second time. That means eyes open, ears open, brain engaged.

Even if they won't or can't teach you, since you're not demanding a high wage, you'll have some time to figure things out. Maybe you can find someone to put questions to before your next work shift.

Don't see much future in washing dishes and

cleaning cat boxes? You're looking at it the wrong way. Skills *generalize*. That means it doesn't really matter what you do, you'll learn many things that will apply to other tasks.

By washing dishes and cleaning cat boxes, you'll learn to organize work and storage spaces, prioritize and schedule tasks, do quality-control inspections, handle hazardous chemicals, evaluate material strength, manage infectious disease vectors, recycle both organic and inorganic substances, and watch for veterinary medical symptoms.

If you're asked to clean the refrigerator, you'll get to figure out food storage temperatures, conditions, and shelf-life. You'll learn about culture organisms: some foods require them (cheese, yogurt), some foods are usable if the organisms are removed (mold on jam), and some foods become very dangerous (meat, vegetables, non-acidic fruits).

And if you learn all you can at every task, people will naturally want to give you more tasks and more responsibilities. That will make your services more and more valuable.

But be humble. Being skillful is grown-up. Showing off or boasting is childish.

Also, you'll find that some people are *against* learning. Learn everything you can *in spite of* them. You can guess how well *they'll* do in a rapidly changing world.

Dangerous!

If the good times of the 20th century keep slipping away, the most dangerous animal on the planet may become even more dangerous. That animal is us. No other creature marks its territory with walls, fences, barbed wire, alarms, and land mines, and protects it with guards, dogs, and guns.

Although a few other animals have occasional clashes between groups, only people have developed "tribal warfare" to a high level of organization and technology. Other creatures can get angry. Only people know how to hate.

That's probably not you, because people also have free choice as individuals. But you have to be ready to deal with other people involved in the usual territorial marking, tribal warfare, and hatred.

Preparation is actually quite simple, whether you fear an advancing army, a gang, or just bored police. Ask yourself, *What are they looking for?* Even if they aren't on a well-defined mission, what kinds of things are they interested in?

1.   Enemies and criminals, of course.   Are you one?   Might you look or sound like one by accident? Enemies are usually identified by uniforms, facial features, or language.   Even if you are a respected citizen, if you happen to look or sound like an invading enemy, you will need to be *very* careful, and might need to avoid public places.   Also, there are many ways we can appear to be a guilty criminal even when we aren't — running, poor posture, a fearful glance, or getting angry at police.

2.   Appearing to "collaborate" (work with) the enemy, or "aid and abet" (help) a criminal, will also get you in trouble.   Remember, it may not matter if the other person *really is* an enemy or criminal.   Give careful thought to which of your meetings, conversations, and exchanges should happen behind closed doors.

3.   Much harder to protect are the many "other things" they might want: weapons, food, shelter, vehicles, fuel, money, valuables, and females.   You can't hide all those things during normal times, but you can avoid bragging or showing them off, especially if you have an unusual amount.   Also, you can start giving thought to what you'll do if times change, and those things are suddenly "magnets" for anyone with the power to take them away from you.

Invisibility

Most of the time, neighbors help each other, police chase bad guys, and firemen put out fires. Occasionally, when everyone's scared and stressed out, they forget how civilization is supposed to work. When that happens, people with power sometimes use it against the wrong people.

It may be hard to predict when that will happen. It could be during a demonstration, a riot, a natural disaster with refugees, a serious revolution, or an actual war. You'll have to use your eyes, ears, and intuition to know when it's time to ... disappear.

Since you can't *actually* disappear, you'll have to use some tricks to make sure you don't look or sound like the kinds of people others are angry at or afraid of. Generally that means appearing harmless, but not weak.

These suggestions are mainly for people not involved in the violence, but even if you have reason to be involved, or can't avoid it, these ideas may help at other times.

Most forms of martial arts training include this idea, and a good example can be found in the movie *Karate Kid*. When a punch is coming your way, "be not there." In other words, the easiest way to avoid damage is to not be in the path of destruction.

In martial arts, this requires quick movement, and not all of us are that quick. But in most situations, clear thinking can substitute for speed.

Forest or brush fire coming your way? A moment of thought about the direction of the wind can save your life. If you are fast, but don't think, you may run in the wrong direction and find yourself surrounded by smoke and flames.

See a gang coming to rob the store you're in? Staring makes you a witness (and therefore the gang's enemy). Screaming makes you a nuisance (to be silenced). Slipping quickly and quietly into the back room, to find the back door or a hiding place, keeps you alive.

Police coming to arrest demonstrators, and you don't want to go to jail? *Walk* away, don't run. Walking has the symbolic meaning of *dis-interest*. Running means *guilty*. But if the police say, "Stop!" then continuing to walk away, or getting angry, means *resisting arrest*, and speaking with them calmly means *innocent bystander*.

Invisibility Ideas

Most dangers in our modern world come from other people in one way or another, and usually they are not, at least at first, directly interested in you. The idea of being "invisible," therefore, is all about sensing what is important to the dangerous people, and noticing where they are focusing their attention. Only then can you "be not there" by being somewhere or something they can't "see."

This is especially challenging for extroverts, "people people," because they naturally want to attract the attention of others to help them solve problems.

But assuming we aren't prepared and equipped to fight our way, Rambo-style, out of a dangerous situation, then we must get it clear in our heads that we're attempting to *not* attract attention, *not* be seen. We can't literally be invisible, like some super-heroes, but we can make ourselves uninteresting.

If the dangerous people are looking for an easy target to shoot at, then you need to be hidden, in the shadows, behind things, wearing dark clothing — you get the idea. But what if the dangerous people *are* looking for someone lurking in the shadows? Change of plan! Now you need to be out in the open, walking tall like you owned the place. See the difference?

Human beings are territorial, and one important way to avoid angering them is to avoid violating their "turf." Understanding and accepting the "turf rules" can save your life. In most cases, the boundaries are defined by something physical like a fence or wall. Or it could subtle, like just grass on the edge of the sidewalk or road. We don't like strangers in our territories, or lingering near the boundaries.

If you pass near a turf boundary too slowly, you'll look like you're "checking it out." If you go too fast, people will think you're fleeing the scene of your latest crime. But if you move at normal speed, acting like you're going somewhere else, suddenly you're "invisible."

Each kind of dangerous person or group has different things they pay attention to. Whenever possible, discuss the dangers in advance with your team.

Like a Super-Hero

"I already used those invisibility ideas, twice I think, during the ice storm!" Ashley announced.

Her 3 friends around the campfire looked at her as if she had just leapt tall buildings in a single bound.

Suddenly Ashley felt embarrassed. "It wasn't any big deal, I just, you know, avoided some things."

Her friends' worshipful expressions changed to friendly smiles.

"First there was this ambulance, with chains on, going slowly down the freeway to get to an accident I could see up ahead. You know, the bike path is right beside the freeway there at 120th Street. They slowed down and looked right at me. I didn't want them to waste time with me since I was fine, so I kept striding along, didn't even look at them after that. They got the message and speeded up to get to the accident."

Jeremy nodded. "Good thinking. If they'd stopped for you, they'd make you go to the hospital, and your parents would have to come get you ..."

"Yeah, all totally useless, just more people sliding around on the ice."

"Did you tell your parents about that?" Rosemary asked with a slight grin.

"No way! It would have given them more ammo."

Rosemary nodded with a smirk.

"Okay," Bobby began, "you're our invisibility teacher. What was the second time?"

"It was more serious. About 11 o'clock some guys were hanging around outside a little grocery store, right on the street I wanted to walk down. They were talking tough, but I couldn't hear what they were saying. It might have been nothing, but my guts started screaming at me."

"What did you do?" Rosemary asked with big, round eyes.

"It all happened in seconds. I heard their voices, felt my guts warning me, and saw a little path that went beside a house. I had no idea where it went, but without a break in my stride, I took it."

"No time to get out a flashlight or *anything*," Jeremy speculated.

"Right. Once I was beside the house, it was so dark I had to feel my way, but no one was following me, so I slowed down, groped along, and came out in an alley behind the house."

"Spooky!" Bobby said in his best Halloween voice.

"I don't make a *habit* of walking down dark alleys in strange neighborhoods during ice storms, but for two blocks, it felt like the right place to be."

More Invisibility

Most of the time, being noisy draws attention, but if most people are making noise, being silent might stick out (if you can be seen). Just be sure to pick the right kind of noise. If everyone else is laughing and you scream — you get the idea.

Good, upright posture is a symbol for "respected citizen," while hunching and slinking means "guilty." If you feel like freaking out, remember that a certain kind of freaking out means "respected citizen in distress," and a slightly different kind means "mentally-ill weirdo." You can practice with your team, and tell each other what you think.

Every society has color codes. Bright colors are usually acceptable for women, not for men. Authority figures wear black or dark blue with white, yellow, or orange lettering or trim. Remember that those authority figures don't like civilians pretending to be one of them, but there are so many kinds of private security people today that the lines have blurred.

Dark colors are best for hiding, if that's what you need to do. Light colors, and especially warm colors, stick out in any natural environment. The natural world is black, brown, and dark green. Our human world is mostly shades of gray.

If you have a bag or purse, is it snatchable? A short strap over one shoulder is easy to snatch, a longer strap over the opposite shoulder is much better. But in any case, a bag means "valuables inside." Are your valuables really inside? Remember that in bad times, a sandwich may be just as interesting to a thief as gold. Be prepared to let go of it — it's not worth your life.

Openly carrying a weapon is NOT an invisibility method. It's an implied dare to others, few people are prepared to use a weapon well, and it will probably attract the attention of police. An umbrella (in a rainy place) or a cane (that you appear to need) might be much more useful, and will avoid negative reactions.

If our world keeps slipping into tougher times, many people will be defiant, trying to hold onto "The American Dream," or whatever you want to call it. There may be times to stand up and do that, and other times when it's too dangerous. You must choose, and the situation may change from moment to moment. "Invisibility" is just one tool in your personal toolbox, among many others.

Lifeboat Ethics

This is the kind of thing everyone hopes they never have to do, but the price of being unprepared is just too high.

Imagine what happens when a lifeboat tries to pick up too many people. It gets lower and lower in the water, then sinks, and everyone dies.

"Lifeboat ethics" apply any time you have to make the gut-wrenching decision to *not* help someone, because if you do, the entire group is hurt, including the person you were trying to help.

The "help" you are tempted to give may even be life-or-death help. But if you do, in a "lifeboat" situation, it means the person dies anyway (maybe a little later), you die, and your entire team dies too.

The decision may seem simple and easy when just thinking about it. The difficulty comes when the person is real, right in front of you, maybe even looking into your eyes. The person might even be a sweet, innocent child. Could you deny them help, even let them die, as a conscious, purposeful choice?

✳

"No!" Ashley wailed. "Not my little sister!"

Jeremy shrugged. "You asked for a hard one."

"Please don't make me choose you guys over her. Anyone else in the world, just not her!"

"So ... are you saying ..." Bobby began, "you'd help her even if it would kill all of us *and* her?"

"I'm saying I'd just be a quivering idiot and couldn't decide."

"Couldn't you just, maybe, do the math?" Jeremy asked. "One death or five."

Ashley thought about it for a long time with a shriveled look on her face. Eventually her friends heard a tiny voice whimper, "no."

✳

Part of being a team is knowing and accepting each other, including our weaknesses and limitations. The rest of Ashley's team now knows that if a "lifeboat" situation ever came up involving her little sister, Ashley would not be able to make that difficult decision, and someone else would have to (probably with Ashley tied up and gagged).

EROEI

"Huh?"

Energy Returned On Energy Invested.

"Oh."

It's the technical term for Hard Cold Reality Coming To Knock. It's the monster that's about to bite us in the ... you know what.

When crude oil was first pumped out of the ground in the late 1800s and early 1900s, we got about 100 barrels of oil for every one barrel it took to fuel the operation. That's an EROEI of 100:1.

Fast forward. Today, the remaining oil is deeper in the Earth, farther away, and often under the ocean. We're getting an EROEI of 30:1 at best, usually 20:1. "Alternative" sources of energy (wind, solar, etc.) operate in the 10:1 to 2:1 area. Making fuel by growing corn is less than 1:1, which means we lose energy (and food) by doing it. Oil from Canadian tar sands may also be less than 1:1.

Welcome to Hard Cold Reality. If it takes more energy than it gives, we're done. It doesn't matter how much oil is left. We won't be able to use it. It's like a vending machine that gives out dollar bills. The amount you have to put in, to get a dollar bill, keeps going up. When it gets to $1, how many people will use it?

But there's another monster at work, called "Peak Oil." When we're pumping oil as fast as we can, as fast as the Earth's geological limits will allow (which has been the case since 2005), and we want a little more, the price skyrockets because the pumping can't respond to the new demand.

The ridiculous new price (up to $147 a barrel in 2008) causes the economy to stall, because everything we do takes oil. We're still trying to recover from that 2008 stall, but aren't having much luck. If we do get the economy going, the price of oil will again knock us back down. It's like hitting our heads against a ceiling.

Our leaders are used to solving problems by talking and throwing money around. A monster called Hard Cold Reality is knocking on our door, it's not listening to our words, doesn't want our money, and won't go away. It growls, "EROEI!"

Our Place in History

We've already talked about the Myth of Progress and other myths we learned when we were young. Another assumption we like to make is that we can do anything, solve any problem, overcome any limitation.

Unfortunately, the fact is that any time our projects get to be a certain size, they fall apart. One of the first examples on record was the Tower of Babel. All through history, when nations get too big, we call them "empires." They seem to be, by their nature, unstable. Many empires have risen, and all have fallen, except the few most recent ones. All of those appear to be past their prime, and are struggling with huge problems.

There's nothing shameful about this. Every creature has things it can do, places it can live, but also limits. We can be proud that we can do more things, and live more places, than any other creature, but it's silly to pretend we don't have limits.

Our limits are probably coded into the genetic

DNA molecules we pass on to our children. They cause us to freak out when we get too hot, too cold, too crowded, too lonely, or a hundred other things. Most limiting of all, they cause us to think and communicate poorly when our projects and empires get too big and complex, like happened at the Tower of Babel.

Right now, a long series of empires, which grew with the help of cheap energy, are all winding down. The Netherlands, France, Great Britain, Germany, Japan, the Soviet Union, the USA, China ...

When empires die, the people don't go away. They just quit trying to rule the world, and have to get used to having fewer goodies. For example, when the western Roman Empire collapsed in the early 400s, the people continued to live their lives and have children, who became today's Italians.

In the 21st century, one more empire will be winding down, the "empire" of corporations and banks that run global trade, which will become very rare because of high energy prices.

Surviving the end of an empire isn't too difficult, as long as you put down roots in your community. If your wealth comes from sunshine, soil, plants, animals, and people who know you, you'll be okay. If your wealth requires government payments, or stocks and bonds from far-away economic activity, you might be in for a big surprise.

The Future

We can only make educated guesses about future trends based on the forces at work in the present. Here are a few to think about:

Low Energy — Energy of all kinds will become scarcer and more expensive. Most of us will have to use much smaller amounts.

Re-Localized — Most of our food and other things will come from very close by (because transportation will be so expensive) or will just be produced at home. Even governments will probably become much more local, such as today's counties and shires. Most people will travel much less, and air transportation (which must use oil) will become extremely expensive.

Police Power — The limits put on the police by laws and courts seem to be weakening. That means we will all have to be very careful about where we are, what we do, and what we say any time police might be watching.

Corporate Power — Corporations appear to be gaining all the rights of citizens, but few of the responsibilities. Also, our governments are handing more and more tasks to corporations that used to be done by government offices. Even though that might save some money, it will probably also lead to more abuses of power.

Climate Change / Global Warming — Hot, dry places are getting hotter and drier. With more power failures, and higher costs for the energy we can get, they may become unlivable. Wet places are getting wetter, causing more floods. Storms, also driven by warmth, are bigger and more frequent.

Diseases and Pests — Following global warming, diseases, insects, and other critters are moving from the tropics into new areas both north and south of the equator, and higher into mountains.

Sea Level — Also because of global warming, sea level all over the world is rising, making coastal areas more vulnerable to storms, and eventually unlivable.

Farmers and Laborers — Today, it takes 10 calories of energy from crude oil and natural gas to make and transport every calorie of food we eat. As the price of energy goes up, human and animal muscle will have to be used again. That means most of us will find that the only jobs available are in the fields as farmers and laborers.

Sleep-Walking?

Most people agree we should protect children from knowledge of "bad" things. There is, however, great disagreement about exactly who is a "child." Some people push for young adults to be considered "children" and kept from all knowledge of anything important.

But it gets worse. A few powerful people have decided that we shouldn't let *anyone* know about important events in the world. These people have their fingers deep into government, banking, newspapers, television, and public education. In some countries, they have almost complete control over the flow of information. Luckily, in most countries, there's still a push-pull contest between the forces of secrecy and the forces of openness. But in recent years, especially since 2001, the secrecy people have been winning.

This struggle is nothing new. People in power always try to keep information to themselves because that increases their power. One negative result is that few people understand the world's problems, so very few people are working to solve them.

To be honest, the problems of the past were fairly small, limited to a kingdom or a small empire, so keeping most of the people uninformed was not a big deal.

The difference today is that the problems we face, and need to solve, are bigger than ever before. They might even be big enough to decide the fate of life on Earth. And yet, there are powerful forces trying to convince people that nothing is wrong — we can go on with "business as usual," wasting, burning, and polluting forever, and nothing will happen.

Only you, the individual young adult, can make sure you are prepared to walk into the future with your eyes open, instead of believing everything you are told (or not told) and just "sleep-walking." The important information is there, but *you* have to sniff it out, and use your intuition to recognize when someone is trying to twist it or hide it. The internet helps a lot, as long as you don't completely trust any one web site or author, just as you should never completely trust any one book or newspaper.

The future, after all, belongs to you, young adults, even more than it does to adults.

Shoveling Bull

"I totally understand!" Jeremy blurted out after finishing the last chapter. "When I look at news articles, I can see 3 or 4 different types. The first type, most of them, are just, *Don't Think About Anything, Just Spend Money and Have Fun!*"

Ashley giggled. "That's the only kind I used to read, before ... I decided I wanted to *live*."

Rosemary squirmed. "I still ... never mind."

Bobby looked at Jeremy intently. "What are the other types?"

"Um ... the next biggest group is, *The Economy Just Needs to Start Growing Again!* And they just keep saying it, day after day, year after year, and they *cannot* get it through their heads that nothing's growing, and nothing's *going* to grow, except weeds."

Bobby chuckled and nodded. "You mean Peak Oil and all that?"

"Yeah. Then there are a few articles that *sound* good at first, but they're just taking tiny bits of change and blowing it up. If something went up 1%, they say it's *soaring*, and down 1%, it's *plunging*, all just to make their point, whatever they already believe."

Ashley laughed. "I've seen that kind."

"Oh, and I just thought of another type, the ones so full of jargon and abbreviations that you have to be an *expert* to figure them out, so there's no way of knowing if they're bull or not."

"I hate that kind," Rosemary said. "They look like Alphabet Soup."

"And finally," Jeremy said with a sigh, "there are a *very few* good news articles that explore things, with a half-way open mind, using words we can read."

Ashley smiled. "Those are the ones I leave open for my parents to see."

＊

Every "side" has a group of "true believers" who write for that side, no matter what happens. Some of them are paid, others just blindly loyal. Their writings have a certain flavor, and can usually be spotted quickly. Other than to get an understanding of that side's "belief system," their writings are not very useful because of their tendency to filter or twist the facts, or just plain lie.

The same people act as "debunkers" against the opposite side. They rarely understand what they are writing against. Again, not very useful.

Our Leaders?

How easy was it for *you* to understand "carrying capacity" and "overshoot"? Can *you* picture how falling "EROEI" and "Peak Oil" have caused our economy to stop growing?

Our leaders aren't scientists, often not even scholars. Sometimes they even get elected because they are (or pretend to be) simple, "folksy" people. They understand the worlds of people and politics (power struggles among people). The problems we are facing come from the worlds of geology and climate science.

The voters who pick our leaders understand even less than our leaders do. When times are tough, leaders get elected who tell the people what they want to hear, what *sounds* like it will be good for the economy and jobs. The best example, a true master of the art, was Adolph Hitler. If times get worse, that type of leader will probably show up again.

Finally, there's money to be made, and power to be gained, during hard times. Throughout most of history, leaders didn't see their jobs as solving problems, but simply as enjoying power. Many still think that way. The idea of a leader as a "civil servant" is quite new, and still fairly rare. People who are rich and powerful are usually skilled at placing themselves just where they need to be to profit from bad times. To them, everything's just fine.

Those are some of the reasons our leaders are unable, or unwilling, to solve the problems facing the 21st century. However, this book does not suggest we put much faith in "political action" because that usually just replaces one set of clueless or corrupt leaders with another set of clueless or corrupt leaders. The fact is, the problems we are facing may be too complex for *anyone* to understand and solve.

It is certainly true that some clear-headed scientists understand ecological overshoot, and some open-minded economists understand Peak Oil. That doesn't mean they would make good leaders, and anyway, people have never shown much desire to elect "brains" when they go to vote.

It's entirely possible that as our lives become re-localized, our leaders on any level above the local community will become nearly useless.

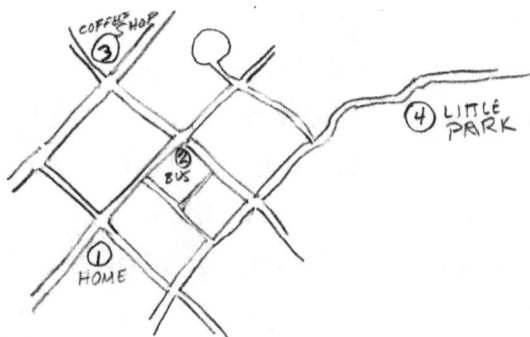

Meeting Places

The kinds of problems that can strike suddenly, like a bad storm or an earthquake, can easily come at the worst possible time, such as when all the members of your family or your team are scattered around town, or even in different towns.

After dealing with immediate dangers, the first thing people want to do at these times is communicate with others they care about, and be with them as soon as possible. Unfortunately, the mobile phone system is very vulnerable to power failures. Land line phones last longer, but a storm can take down the wires. Fallen trees and poles can block roads, and too many cars can cause all traffic to slow to a crawl.

At times like this, *fear* and *desperation* are common, and *clear thinking* becomes rare. To add to the danger, many of the people experiencing fear and desperation are driving cars.

When the lines of communication and transportation are broken, it's too late to make a plan. Everyone, with panic close, must guess what they should do, and what other family or team members will do. The world becomes filled with people trying to find each other, but usually not succeeding because they're all doing it at once, and all without a plan.

Your team is smarter than that, right?

One very good method for dealing with this situation is to agree on 3 to 5 meeting places. Place #1 is your most protected "home base," with each higher number farther away. Each team member, in a disaster situation, goes to the lowest-numbered place they can get to, and leaves a message if they move on.

Shelter, a comfortable place to sit, a pay telephone, and a 24-hour restaurant with good hamburgers and milk shakes, would all be nice at each meeting place, but are not essential. What is important is that you can wait there, all day and all night if necessary, without being forced to leave for any reason. Also, there must be a place to leave messages that team members can find, but hopefully not other people. Consider how those messages will survive if it's raining or windy.

With a plan like this, you'll have a much higher chance of finding each other again, or at least knowing what happened, than most people.

Dog Poop

A clear sky brought a chill to the air as soon as the sun set. The team of four huddled close to their little campfire.

"Place #1 is here or any of our houses," Ashley stated. "If we can get to any of them, we're as good as home, and it's easy to walk around and check them, even if the phones are history."

Jeremy looked thoughtful. "I think about 2 more places should do it."

Ashley nodded.

"Bulletin board at the Post Office," Bobby suggested.

Jeremy shook his head. "Closed at night, and they

don't allow personal messages."

Ashley looked up at the stars. "Yeah, must be all-day, all-night kinds of places. Places ... no one cares about. Like ... under the loading dock behind the grocery store ..."

Jeremy's eyes opened wide. "Perfect! There are always boxes and milk crates under there, easy to hide, sheltered from the rain ..."

"But," Rosemary began in a sour voice, "there could be dog poop under there."

Ashley chuckled. "It's just for emergencies, when you wouldn't *care* about dog poop. And there's food nearby, and a phone in front of the store."

"Okay," Jeremy said, finding it on his city map, "that's our meeting place for town. Now we need one about half-way here."

The crackling of the fire was the only sound as they all thought about it.

"I know!" Bobby suddenly blurted out. "That big box at the beginning of our road!"

"Telephone junction box," Jeremy clarified.

"We can write messages on it," Bobby added. "No one would notice with all the other graffiti."

Ashley nodded. "And there's woods behind it where we can hide and keep out of the wind. I've crept around in them while my dad was changing a tire."

Rosemary shriveled her nose. "Any ... dog poop?"

Your Money

This chapter is about *money*, not about *wealth*. Many people think that money = wealth, but that's not completely true, and sometimes it's not true at all. We'll talk about wealth soon.

I was taught, when little, that keeping money at home, in cash, was *terrible*. Whether or not that was true then (it was certainly true for the banks!), today you might find reasons to keep your money closer.

Remember Murphy's Law? Bad things always happen at the worst possible times. Some bad things can be fixed, or made more bearable, with money. In most places today in the USA, $10 will get you a meal, and $100 will get you a hotel or motel room.

But not all ways of paying for things work the same.

Want to use a debit or credit card? That requires the telephone lines or the internet, maybe both, to be working smoothly, and the computers of the card company, maybe also your bank, to be up and running. And, of course, there must be enough money in your account (debit cards) or line of credit (credit cards).

Want to write a check? That's just a promise to pay later, written on paper. How are you going to prove to someone, during an emergency, that your promise is good? The only reliable uses of checks are to pay rent and utility bills.

Cash talks. Cash can be used by whoever holds it, so as soon as you hand it to someone, they *feel* paid, and are happy to give you what you need. The risk of counterfeit money is very small, and devices to detect it are cheap, so any business can test your cash on the spot if they want to.

The only remaining risk is trying to buy something small with a large bill. No matter how much cash you carry, always have some small bills.

Cash can, of course, be stolen. If you're going to keep much at home, a good hiding place is necessary, but it should allow you to get to your money quickly, and without letting others know your hiding place. Paper money can mold if it gets wet, and can be eaten by insects and rodents. A jar and lid will take care of both dangers.

Banks

Banks have been around for thousands of years, starting as simple "money changers" in the marketplace. They provide some services that might be useful, and charge for those services one way or another.

For young adults, it's best to avoid them. Get paid, for things you do or sell, in cash whenever possible. If the person must write a check, make sure it's from a local bank. A check drawn on an out-of-town bank might be useless to you, unless you take the time and expense of traveling to that town.

Our regular employment system is set up so you almost have to use banks. When someone pays you with a check, you will need a bank to change that check into money.

It varies from state to state, and bank to bank, but generally banks don't like doing business with minors, unless their parents are involved, so they can go after them if the check is bad. But since this book is about standing on your own two feet ...

Normally, banks will cash *their* checks for people without an account who have plenty of ID, but they may not be very nice about it, and may even finger-print you. For a minor, *if* you have a state ID card *and* a passport, and it's a payroll check from a *local* business, or from someone they *know* and can call, *and* you are very patient, they *might* cash a check for you. It's best to try at the actual *branch* of the check-writer, not just the right bank. Don't forget to act and speak totally grown-up.

If you do that regularly, and they get to know you and never have any problems, they *might* let you open a savings account without your parents involved (if state law allows it). Know the service charges! You might need a minimum balance to avoid a monthly fee. Don't be impressed by promises of interest, as it will probably be next to nothing. In most cases, they take dollars and toss you pennies. Do the math and always know what's in your account.

Not Banks

Banks will dangle many tempting things in your face when (maybe before) you turn 18. Keep your money in an account, and you'll earn interest! Get an ATM, debit, or credit card! Take out a loan to buy a car or go to college!

For young adults dealing with the bad economy of 2012 and beyond, all those tempting things are dangerous. Most of them are designed to make your money easier to spend, in other words, harder to save. That may be the last thing you need. Also, every transaction has a fee. It may be charged to you directly, or it may be charged to the other person, such as a business you are buying something from. The business passes the fee along, by charging higher prices, to you.

If you over-draw your bank account by writing checks or using a debit card, the fees are large. You might say, "I'll be careful and never over-draw." The fact is, keeping good records and "balancing a checkbook" is beyond most people, and that's how banks make money.

Banks also make money by loaning it out. That means they don't "keep" the money that's in your account. Sometimes the loans go bad (especially during — you guessed it — bad times). If that happens too much, a bank can go out-of-business. In most countries, the government insures bank accounts and they will *probably* give you your money *someday*.

If you open a bank account of any kind, consider the money in it unusable for any emergency. Some of it may disappear for service charges you didn't know about. The bank may be closed when you need your money. ATMs can run out of cash, or be down because of power failures. Also, the government can order banks to close at any time.

For some of the same reasons, a box in a bank vault is *not* the right place to keep anything you might need in an emergency. Also, the government can decide to take any gold or silver it can get its hands on, which has happened in the USA once before. Bank vault boxes are one of the first places they'd look.

Out of Debt!

Owing money to someone else is the opposite of standing on your own two feet. It's a burden and a worry, physically and mentally, every day (even if you only make monthly payments). It's a "fish hook" in your flesh, with someone else on the other end of the string. And, of course, that other person can usually take back whatever you bought with the money (house, car, etc.) if you don't keep paying.

When hard times come, people in debt are the first to lose everything. Millions of people have been losing their homes in "foreclosures" since the economy stalled in 2008. Part of standing on your own two feet is totally owning, without debt, however much or little you have. Only then do you truly know what you have. A tent that you own will be there when you need it, and a nice house with a "mortgage" may not be.

Some people argue that when there's inflation, people with debt come out ahead. That's only true if (A) your income is rising, or (B) the value is rising of the things you went into debt for. It's hard to find a person whose income is rising today, and our inflation is a special kind called "stagflation." During stagflation, energy and food prices rise, but houses, cars, and jobs go down. Most debt is for houses and cars, so the inflation won't help.

Your parents probably went into debt for their house and car. This is not your debt, but you should know about it, because it could mean that those things will disappear someday. Be kind when you ask them about it. They simply did what everyone was doing to have a house and a car.

But *your* life is yours to make decisions about, regardless of what your parents did. Credit cards, mortgages, and car loans can be very dangerous in hard times. They steal from the future, your future. They only make sense if you are *very sure* the future is going to be wonderful, and you'll have plenty of money.

If you think that, then you haven't been paying much attention to what's going on in the world.

Wheels

Jeremy didn't exactly slither along the ground, like a slug, as he approached the campfire circle, but he might as well have. His friends could tell something was very wrong.

Ashley sat a little closer than usual and poked him. "No suicides allowed at campfire. What's wrong?"

Shame had replaced Jeremy's usual happiness and confidence. "My dad ... they took his truck."

Everyone remained silent.

"He didn't tell me ... he didn't tell *anyone* ... he was behind on payments. He just pretended ..."

Bobby nodded.

"We came out of the grocery store, and there ..." Jeremy paused to swallow the lump in this throat. "... there was the repo guy, a locksmith, and a sheriff ..."

Jeremy started crying softly. Ashley was torn for a moment, then put a hand on his knee.

After wiping his face on his sleeves, the boy found his voice again, this time colored with anger. "They wouldn't even let him have his tool box! Said that since they sent him a letter demanding repossession, the truck was now stolen property!"

Jeremy breathed deeply to collect himself. "My go-bag was in it too, but nothing very valuable. I'll be able to put a new one together in a week or two."

"Good," Rosemary whispered.

"I don't want to talk about it anymore," Jeremy announced, and they turned their attention to marshmallows and other lighter concerns.

Ashley talked about her work at Mrs. White's house, Rosemary mentioned some people she knew that might be good on the team, and Bobby shared another good meeting place he had discovered.

"I'm gonna save up for a sturdy mountain bike," Jeremy suddenly said during a quiet moment. "It might take years, because I'm gonna have all the money in my hands before I even *look* at them — they can be $1000 or more. It's gonna have plenty of luggage racks and bags, a tool kit, and a basket in front for my go-bag ..."

Ashley nodded and smiled, feeling the determination in her friend to never, ever get caught in the debt trap.

Wealth!

Most people just think wealth is money. Wealth is actually anything that has *material value* to someone. Normally, that includes money, because money can be exchanged for things you need or want. But money can die, as you'll learn about soon, so money is not *always* wealth.

There are really 3 different kinds of wealth:

Primary Wealth — all the material stuff we use directly: food, clothing, fuel, medicine, tools and machines we use at home, houses, land, etc.

Vocational Wealth — all the things we use to make money: tools of our trades, business inventory, commercial real estate, etc.

Symbolic Wealth — all the wealth we print on paper or stamp on coins: money, titles to real estate or vehicles, debt notes, postage stamps, etc.

We use *primary wealth* directly to live and be

happy. That's what your go-bag, your deep pantry, and your robust medical kit are all about.

We can only use *vocational wealth* if conditions in the world allow us to follow our trades, crafts, or businesses. If you are a plumber, normally you can trade your skills for money, then spend the money. But if a heavy snow keeps you at home, you can't eat your pipe wrenches, nor build a fire with them.

Our *symbolic wealth* is even further from having any direct use. We can't eat it, and it won't even (by itself) fix your plumbing. It's only useful if our complex *marketplaces* are working, AND we agree with the other person in the marketplace on the value of our printed paper or coins. The grocery store might be open, and it might have plenty of bread, but if I think bread should be $2, and the grocery store wants $4, I will go home without bread. We didn't agree on the value of my *symbolic wealth*.

All 3 types of wealth are important, but conditions in the world may force us to move wealth from one category to another (or make us wish we had). If the world economy is growing (like it was from 1985-2005), *symbolic wealth* may be very profitable. If we have a skill or business that is in demand, we will probably invest more in our *vocational wealth*. If natural disasters, civil unrest, and other "in your face" problems start piling up, *primary wealth* becomes essential.

Can Money Die?

Yes, and it has happened many times. When money loses its value slowly, we call it "inflation." It takes wealth away from people who work and save.

When a government needs more money than it can collect from taxes, or borrow, it can just *make* more money to spend. That leads to inflation, then "hyper-inflation," when money loses its value so quickly that normal business isn't possible.

Imagine needing a wheel-barrow to take enough money to the store for a loaf of bread. But hurry! Tomorrow, that loaf will cost 2 wheel-barrows full of money.

If you don't prepare, you could find yourself holding $100 bills that are only good for starting campfires. Preparation is easy. It will cost you something, but you'll probably make a profit, even if hyper-inflation never comes.

Gold and silver keep their value when money dies. In early 2012, gold is about $1600 an ounce, and silver is about $30 (in US dollars). Tenth ounce coins are usually the smallest, so they cost about $170-$180 for gold, $3-$4 for silver (the seller adds a mark-up, usually 5%-10%). Most young adults can afford the silver, and it will be the most useful coin for buying little things like food.

In the USA, dimes from 1964 and earlier are 90% silver. You can't find them in change you get, you have to buy them at a coin shop.

It's impossible to predict what the prices of gold and silver will do, but they've been going up for years, as the value of dollars, euros, and other kinds of money goes down (inflation). But if hyper-inflation comes along, the important thing will not be exactly how much money gold and silver coins are worth, but that they'll be worth *something*, when money isn't.

Most people will *not* prepare in this way. They will just refuse to believe that money can die. If hyper-inflation happens, they will have to bring piles of $100 bills to the store. With your little silver dime, you will have a much higher chance of getting food.

You should start now. If your budget is tight, putting $3 or more each week into one tiny silver dime may be the hardest thing you've ever done.

[A 1964 or earlier silver dime contains .07234 troy ounces of silver, and a quarter contains .18084 troy ounces of silver. If you can afford it, consider the new US Silver Eagles, 1986-today, one troy ounce of silver, currently $35-$40.]

Rosemary's Wealth

After starting the campfire, with Ashley handing her twigs and advice, Rosemary wore a proud smile as she pulled a plastic tube of dimes from her go-bag.

The other three members of her team noticed that her go-bag was much lighter, with no cans of beans bulging from the sides.

"Cool!" Bobby said, taking the tube of silver coins. "Your first full tube! Mine's about 3/4 full."

Rosemary grinned. "And I already have another tube, ready for its first dime after I do some yard work on Saturday."

Ashley received the tube from Bobby and hefted it. "Fifty silver dimes. That ought to be worth *something!*"

"I kept a list," Rosemary responded, "of what I paid for them. Came to $179*, and I could sell them, right now, for $217*. But I won't!"

"Good," Jeremy said, returning the tube of precious metal to its owner. "They'll be worth much more someday."

Bobby nodded. "My parents asked me what I wanted for my birthday. I said silver dimes. They pooh-poohed the idea. So I said I'd gladly get a *gold coin!*"

Ashley and Jeremy laughed. Rosemary smiled as she slipped her precious tube of silver into the secret inside pocket of her go-bag.

✳

*   These numbers are just an example of what the situation might be at one point in time, with the price of silver moving from $40 to $60 per ounce. The numbers you get will be different.

You will probably notice that the prices of silver and gold are constantly changing, and when they go down a little, you might feel bad, and be tempted to sell it all and quit. That, of course, is exactly what other investors want, because then they can buy *yours* at that lower price. Be patient, and remember that it's not silver and gold changing value. They've been worth almost exactly the same for thousands of years. It's the value of *money* going up and down (usually down).

Home Sweet Home?

You'll probably say you can't do anything about where you live. You're probably right. For most young adults, it's decided by where their parents work, rent or own a home, or own a business.

But you need to ask yourself this hard question, so if things turn ugly, you'll at least be mentally prepared:

If all "imported" supplies fail, can your family (and your team) survive at your current location?

"Imported" supplies include electricity that comes from the wires, city water, piped gas, and food from grocery stores.

What does that leave? Your own garden, farm, or ranch. Water from a well (hand-pumped), spring, stream, river, or lake. Firewood your family cuts. Food and other things produced by your local community that they will sell or trade.

Also, take some time to think about what it means to "survive" — water, something to eat, warm clothing, and a roof over your head. It's not the same as having a freezer full of pizza pockets and ice cream. "Survive" means the minimum. Some climates do not give us what we need to survive all year long, but by saving up the bounty of summer, we can get through the winter.

We've talked about the need for community and other things that go beyond the essentials of life, but basic survival comes first. The decision to relocate to a more survivable place might have to be made quickly, so you'd probably have to consider just survival, and trust that the other things can be found later.

If the answer to the huge question above is *no*, do you have any friends or relatives whose home *is* survivable without "imported" supplies? We are, of course, talking about friends or relatives who would let you in the door and add you to their household, not "acquaintances," "cyber-friends," or "fair-weather friends."

Okay, you know the score. There's probably nothing else you can do about it right now. You just need to know, and share your answer with your team.

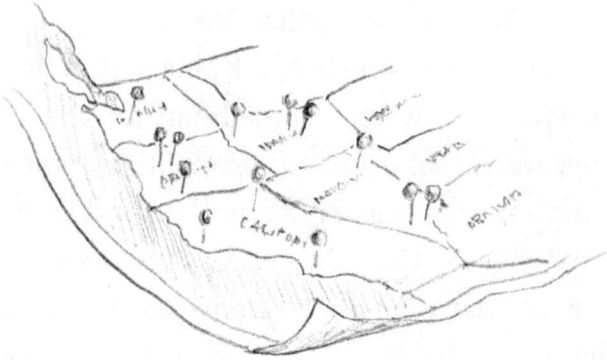

Bad News?

"I got those numbers," Rosemary said as soon as she sat down on a log.

The others could tell by the look on her face that she wasn't happy about it.

"Summer's nice ..." she began with a sigh.

"We know," Bobby mumbled.

She flashed him a frown. He cringed.

"Winter is the problem," Rosemary went on. "Almost 40 inches of rain, 67 days with lows below freezing, and 21 days with highs below freezing! It's a death trap here!"

Jeremy could see that Rosemary was being very serious, so he kept his mouth shut.

Ashley thought about how to proceed. "What

happens if we go one state east?"

Rosemary shrugged.

Jeremy reluctantly raised his hand. "I have an uncle over there, and they have a joke. There are only 2 days a year that you don't get either heat stroke or frostbite, one in the spring, one in the fall. I think it's about the same to the north, maybe worse."

"And one state south?"

Bobby knew. "I have a cousin down there. It's either burning desert or frozen mountains. Most wells are a thousand feet deep. Electric bills are *ridiculous.*"

"Oh," Rosemary whispered, looking at the ground.

"I've heard you can garden here all year long," Jeremy said to no one in particular, "as long as you don't mind Brussels sprouts and things like that."

Rosemary made a face.

"Our creek never freezes," Bobby added. "Some places, *everything* freezes solid in the winter!"

After a long silence, Rosemary took a deep breath, but wasn't quite ready to look at her team mates. "Maybe ... it's not so bad here ..."

"I know what we need to do," Ashley announced. "We need to find someone who lives without electricity and all that stuff, and visit them."

"I think my dad knows someone," Jeremy began, "way up the valley about 10 miles. They have a cabin, goats, a garden, and the river's crystal clear up there."

Voluntary Poverty

One of the most powerful tricks people have discovered, for getting ready for hard times, is to live like those times are already here, even before you have to.

It may sound weird, until you realize you're doing that any time you go hiking or camping. People pay lots of money to send their kids to "summer camp." Others rent "rustic cabins" for vacations, or buy places as crew members on old-fashioned sailing ships. Living simply, with little technology, in challenging situations, makes us grow quickly and focus on what's truly important: food and shelter, health and safety, and good relations with other people and animals.

If your team decides to build that good reputation we've talked about, mostly by working for other people with little concern for pay, you'll be taking a giant step toward getting ready. If you put most of your spending money into silver coins and a deep pantry, you'll be making another giant step.

In our story, Ashley and her friends talk around a campfire. Most modern people don't know *how* to build a campfire, even on a pleasant summer evening. In the dark, wind, rain, or snow, it's much harder, but your life may depend on it someday.

One of the best activities for getting ready for the future, physically and mentally, is backpacking. Since you must carry everything, but what the environment can give (usually water and firewood), it forces you to become very aware of what you need ... and what you don't need.

You can start in your own back yard, as long as you accept the one rule of the game: you only get what you can carry in one trip. Your first "backpacking trip" might include a huge armload of stuff, but no one will be watching (except maybe your parents, who will just smile). Eventually, with some experience, the wisdom it brings, and a good frame pack you got for your birthday or whenever, you'll graduate to a sleek load you can carry for miles before making camp.

Any kind of "voluntary poverty" experience lets you get used to "roughing it" while your mistakes are non-fatal. When hard times really arrive, the world will not be so forgiving of your mistakes.

Angel or Reptile?

Most of the time, we float through our daily routines being "civilized people." We say "please" and "thank you," we pay for things at the store, stop at red lights, etc. That civilized behavior is possible because we're well-fed, we have a home, and the police take care of the bad guys.

Take away some of those "nice" things that make civilization possible, and something strange happens.

Inside each of us is a "reptile," a simple creature who is concerned only with personal safety, food, and sex. When civilization goes away, our "reptile" usually comes out, and is not afraid to run away, or fight to the death, to get its basic needs met.

Inside each of us is also an "angel," a being who wants to help others and cooperate with *everyone*, even in the middle of a crisis. That "angel" is even willing to risk death to save others.

Which are we? We have the "wiring" and "programming" for both, and can even swing back and forth quickly. We have the choice, although it may not feel like a conscious choice when danger and confusion are swirling around us (screams, blood, trees falling, sirens, yelling, crying, gun shots — you know).

Our "reptile" isn't perfectly adapted to life because we can't think very far ahead when consumed by fear, anger, and other strong emotions. We elect leaders who become dictators, we fear anyone who is different in any way (like skin color), and we see everything as "us against them" battles.

Our "angel" isn't perfect either, perhaps letting a friend die instead of finding the courage to stop the bad guy, or forming a committee to discuss a problem that needs a quick decision.

Young people can get to know both their "reptile" and their "angel" by experiencing things that are outside their "comfort zones." Difficult sports, camping, hiking 10 miles in the rain, going a day without food, communicating without speaking or writing ... the list is different for each person. By testing yourselves in "uncivilized" situations, and getting to know your reactions to them, you'll have more choice and more personal power when a *real* uncivilized situation comes along.

Good Boundaries

As a mental health therapist who's seen all kinds of mixed-up people, I'm going to give you a special gift by telling you the one thing that most often separates mentally healthy from mentally sick people.

You guessed it, good boundaries.

Needless to say, being mentally healthy will *really* help you survive and be happy in any bad times that come along. And it will help you be on a team and have friends, because we're talking about *inter-personal* boundaries, after all.

Having good boundaries starts with simple, old-fashioned *respect*. Every person wants to be respected in their personal business and personal space unless they *invite* someone else to come in, or someone offers and they *accept*.

Both parents and young people often have trouble with boundaries. It's very easy for either one to forget that the other is a person too. Employers and employees, leaders and followers, rich people and poor people, boys and girls, the majority and the minority ... all have long histories of one kind treating the other kind as an object, instead of a person.

Objects are things. We "own" them, do with them what we want, treat them however we want, tell them what to do, take them, use them, throw them away.

People have feelings and rights. They have a territory we must not enter without permission, or they'll think we're *trying* to bother them. Sometimes it's just a few feet across, as in a store or on the sidewalk. Sometimes it's much bigger, as when driving a car. When I'm flying a helicopter, my "personal space" is about a mile in every direction.

People have feelings about much more than physical space. We all have a keen sense of when someone is sticking their nose in our business. Respect is all about knowing what's our business, what isn't, and asking very politely any time we are tempted to cross the line. "Yes" means *be careful*. "No" means *no*.

How do you learn good boundaries? Like anything: choose to, then practice. Watch other people to see what bothers them. Pay attention to what bothers *you*. Then decide what kind of person you want to be, mentally healthy, or ...

Not Your Business!

Jeremy though for a moment. "My little brother stole something from the store, and I ... didn't stop him."

Ashley immediate pulled her phone out of her go-bag. "Hello, police? Jeremy's brother stole something. I don't know what yet, but it was probably huge ..."

Jeremy smiled, knowing there was no mobile phone reception at their campfire circle.

"You're going to HELL!" Rosemary nearly screamed. "The minister at my church SAID SO!"

Jeremy pouted, just for a second.

"You can't be on our team anymore," Bobby declared with a frown. "We don't want to be *associated* with criminals."

"Ouch!" Jeremy admitted. "That was the worst. Right now, I'd feel really lost without you guys."

The other three smiled with pride.

"What'd he steal?" Ashley asked.

"A grape ... that was on the floor."

The entire team howled with laughter as Ashley ripped open a package of marshmallows.

✳

Ashley took a deep breath. "A boy smiled at me at school today ..."

"What was his name?" Jeremy asked, voice dripping with jealousy.

"He kissed you, didn't he?" Rosemary prodded.

Bobby was chuckling and trying to think. "Um ... did you sleep with him?"

"Of course she did!" Rosemary blurted. "Ashley sleeps with *all* the boys!"

By this time, Ashley was beet-red.

"What are we going to do with a pregnant girl on our team?" Jeremy wondered aloud. "We'll have to make a rule about that ..."

"STOP IT!" Ashley suddenly screamed. "I *hate* this. I don't want to do it anymore."

After a long silence, Jeremy spoke softly. "You were *supposed* to hate it."

Ashley breathed deeply a few more times. "I know. I just didn't realize how terrible it would feel. I hope I never make any of you feel that way ..."

Bobby gathered his courage in the silence that followed. "Almost never."

Reality Levels

Getting a clear understanding of the 3 main levels of reality can really help when you're trying to figure out what's important, what's dangerous, and what's bull ... you know.

Things — atoms, molecules, energy, etc. This includes our bodies, air, water, food, the Earth, sunshine, stars, books, and the ink on the pages. This is the realm of all things *physical*.

Meanings — only accessible by *mind*, it includes everything we would call *information* and *feelings*, such as ideas, words, symbols, numbers, pictures, emotions, and opinions. This is the level of all things *social*, like culture and politics.

Values — only accessible by the higher functions of mind (sometimes called "spirit"), this level is about the "important stuff" contained in *meanings*. A being that can think at this level is called "sapient*." This level includes *spiritual* concepts.

Your computer is a *thing* of plastic, metal, etc. These words on your screen or printed paper have *meanings* (you could define each word, even phrases and sentences). Finally, this entire chapter has *value* in that it explains the three main levels of reality.

One level of reality can *influence* another level, but cannot control it directly.

If someone sends you a letter that says, "You are going to die!" that statement has *meaning* and causes *feelings*. But only the *physical* level of reality can directly cause you to die. "Sticks and stones ..." You know the saying.

If we take a vote, and everyone agrees that 2 + 2 equals 5, we have expressed a *social meaning*. However, nothing in the *physical* world will care, and our vote only holds *value* in that it reveals something about our intelligence.

If a newspaper says, "The unemployment rate is 10%," the *meaning* of that statement is simple. "10%" means 10 out of every hundred. But if you know for a fact that 20% of the people are unemployed, the newspaper's statement suddenly lacks *value*.

If someone, or even everyone, holds the *opinion* that gasoline should be $2 a gallon, the oil companies may still be unable to *physically* produce it for less than $4 a gallon.

✳

* Often, especially in Science Fiction, the word "sentient" is used for the same thing. However, a worm is sentient (can sense its environment), but probably can't think about *values*. You can.

Is This a Test?

Let's imagine, just for a moment, that the universe is run by some form of intelligence. Most people think so, and call that intelligence "God."

Let's further imagine that God has to, at some point, test his "children" (us people) to see if they should go to "college," just get a simple "job," or perhaps are "disabled" and will need on-going care long after other "children" have left "home."

What might God do to test his "children"?

I'm talking about a test that would apply to an entire "people" (species, race, nation, whatever), and not to individuals. We know very well that within a species, individuals grow up at different rates, and achieve different levels of ability and maturity.

This test, ideally, would tempt us with something like "candy," something that immature children can't resist, but mature young adults and older adults can.

There would be only a small amount of this "candy." God does not want us to have it forever, because it's not good for us. It's just there for the purpose of the test. We'll have "good food" after the test, but most of the "candy" will be gone. There might be a little left for special occasions, but not enough to gorge ourselves on.

To make the test more challenging, God has hidden some of the "candy" in places that are very hard to get to. It won't just run out, it'll become more and more difficult to find. We'll have to dig up our "gardens" and tear down our "houses" to get it all.

Are you starting to get an idea of what this "candy" might be?

Just as for individuals, there might be a different future in store for the "children" of God who can out-grow their craving for "candy" at the end of childhood, compared to those who wait until much later in life, if ever, to grow up.

Young adults today can take responsibility for themselves by out-growing their cravings for various kinds of "candy," but they cannot take responsibility for their entire nation, race, or species. It may be that some individuals pass the test, but we, as a whole people, do not. In that case, young adults can look for opportunities to grow and prosper *in spite of* the choices made by other people, their groups, leaders, and governments.

[In the author's opinion, this "candy" is cheap and plentiful energy: coal, oil, gas, and uranium.]

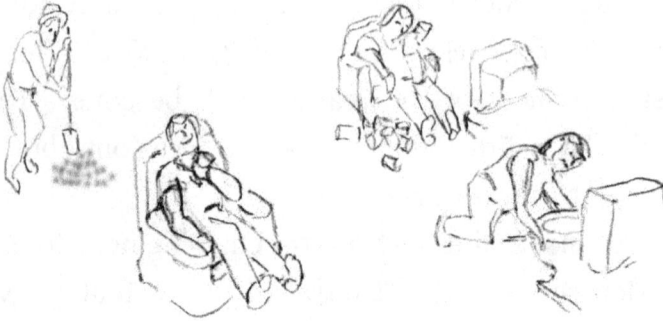

Lullabies

"Lullabies" are all those things we use to help us relax and maybe even fall asleep: drugs, distractions, entertainments.

It's completely natural to want some "lullabies" so we won't feel the *sting* of the hard things in life (work, danger, pain, conflict, fear, confusion). From the way the world is going, it looks like there will be plenty of that stuff in our future.

So we have two choices. We can use the "lullabies" to help us relax after a hard day. Or we can use them to *avoid* the day completely.

When we relax after a hard day, we feel good. We got some things done, solved a problem or two, avoided some things that were better avoided, and moved a little closer to our goals. Now we deserve a little treat from that special shelf in our deep pantry.

But after a day of *avoiding* life, our problems have piled up deeper, and we are further from our goals.

Also, all those "lullabies" probably cost a bunch of money, now gone. We feel ... empty and powerless.

Many things can be used (in moderation) to relax, or (in excess) to avoid life: recreational drugs (like alcohol), unhealthy food, socializing and partying, sex, sleep, hobbies, TV and movies, games, surfing the web, chatting and texting ... just about anything.

The important decision, in each person's hands, is how you want to feel after the "lullabies" wear off, and you have to deal with the real world again.

⁕

Let's glance at a family of about a hundred years ago, which might look like *your* family in 10 or 20 years if energy keeps getting more expensive:

Everyone's up with the sun to care for animals, do chores, and get breakfast cooking. Soon a bell rings and you dash inside for hotcakes. Then the children have lessons while the adults work in the gardens.

Lunch is tasty bean and barley burritos, then the afternoon is filled with productive work in the barn or family room, preparing food products or crafts to sell. Everyone, who is out of diapers, helps in some way.

A burst of cackling from the chicken coop announces a special dinner, and a couple of young adults volunteer to do the plucking. After evening chores, someone gets out a guitar, 2 or 3 board games appear, and grandpa brings out a little bottle of something he brewed last winter.

To Be Refugee?

A refugee is a person, usually along with hundreds or thousands of others, who crawls in from a bad situation (usually a natural disaster or war) and begs for refuge.

History is filled with stories of refugees being treated badly. It's not always on purpose, as the situations that cause people to need refuge usually also cause the entire area to be in shock. When the regular citizens are scrambling to find food, water, medical care, and other needs, it's difficult for them to also help strangers.

In addition, when a disaster strikes, many people look for someone to blame and take their frustrations out on. Refugees are an easy target because they are "outsiders," even if they're from only 10 miles away.

Refugees are usually herded into some large

building or fenced-in area to keep them from interfering with the lives of the normal residents. If the space gets too crowded, that's too bad. Supplies can easily run low, and sanitation can be poor. Diseases spread quickly in those conditions.

You may want to consider avoiding the experience of being a refugee if you have *any* alternative (short of death). Crawling home through the woods, at night, in the rain and mud, is probably more fun. If you have some preparations in place, like a go-bag, meeting/message places, and people in your community who know you, you'll probably be much better off if you *don't* follow the crowd after some disaster.

Following the crowd is, of course, very easy, especially when you're tired, hungry, cold, wet, and maybe in pain from an injury. At those times, it's hard to think. But the fact is, a crowd of people, like a stampede of cattle, may have no idea where it's going, and it might be the worst possible direction. Some ideas:

Ask a few people where they're going, and what good that will do. Think about their answers.

Follow the crowd *at a distance*, and see where it goes and how it's treated before you get *inside* anything you can't get out of.

Breathe slowly, listen to your instincts, and make decisions with your head.

Religion

Religion is about certain organizations (churches, synagogues, temples, etc.), their members, teachings, and politics.

Spirituality is about the growth of the spirit, soul, or whatever you want to call it, inside each person. Many things in this book touch upon spirituality. The process of preparing for difficult times, and remaining happy both before and after those times arrive, will teach you much more.

Religion can be a powerful, positive force in a community, especially during hard times. Churches usually teach, and sometimes actively organize, cooperation among their members, charity toward poor members, and some degree of preparation for future problems. Churches will naturally form community "centers," especially if the economy keeps getting worse, as they're used to operating on tight budgets with volunteer labor.

In the future, you may find good reasons to go to church, even if you never did during good times. It may be an excellent place to make friends, find new team members, learn useful skills, join cooperative projects that let you take something home (like garden produce), and hear of work you might be able to do.

On the other hand, some churches just funnel everything to the minister, or send it to far-away places to support missionaries.

Then there's the thorny issue of *belief*. All churches have an official "belief system," although some keep it vague and general, while others go into great detail. You'd have to listen to this belief system every time you went. You might like it, you might not. You'd have to listen respectfully, or go home.

Some churches require you to *profess* (openly agree with) the belief system. Sometimes it's just words mumbled during a prayer, elsewhere you might have to sign your name in their book.

Some people, during hard times, have made the difficult choice to *pretend* to like the belief system of the dominant religion in their community in order to help them survive. There have even been times and places where that's been necessary to avoid prison or death. You'll have to size up the situation in your location, maybe see how the available religions feel, and make a decision that works for you.

Public Education?

It's hard to imagine public schools completely ceasing to exist, isn't it? But we've only tried educating *everyone* for the last couple of centuries, during the time of cheap energy. For most of history before that, you had to be very rich, or very lucky, to get an education. With the time of cheap energy ending, we might have to go back to that old system.

It's actually not that big a problem. There was a time when few people knew anything, even how to read and write. Today, almost everyone, including young adults, know more than scholars of old. In the future, even if there's no government money available, any family or community that wants to educate its children can easily do so.

What *won't* be possible is teaching hundreds of kids, whether they want to learn or not, all at the same time, in one huge building. That requires administration, security, maintenance, and a large team of professional teachers who have college training with programmed learning systems and complex disciplinary techniques. In other words, it requires lots of money.

Education, like most everything else, will become re-localized as the world becomes poorer. A small community that chooses to teach its children to read, for example, just needs a living room, a literate teenager who likes working with children, and a shelf of story books. Behavior problems will be few, as the alternative will be helping in the gardens, fields, animal pens, or workshops where the rest of the family or community is at work.

During hard times, the subjects people need to learn will be a little different. Rocket science will not be so important. Knowledge that leads to successfully growing food will come first. Healing arts of all kinds will shine, as well as knowing how to maintain whatever machines we still have.

Young adults like you, who are already educated, will be in the best possible position to make this happen. In your community, you may or may not have the help of an adult teacher. Most adults will be very busy trying to hold onto jobs and other things that are slipping away.

Just as with your team, you may have to begin the process of educating the next generation by sitting around a campfire.

Ashley's Path

"Thanks for letting me borrow this old pharmacopeia book," Ashley said as the team settled around the campfire and she handed the little book back to Jeremy. "I photocopied the whole thing."

"Wow," he remarked. "It really spoke to you! Are you going to be a doctor?"

Ashley thought for a moment. "I don't think that's gonna be possible anymore, unless you're rich. But maybe ..." She pulled 4 used books from her go-bag and spread them out in the firelight: emergency medical care, medicinal herbs, first-aid for soldiers, and home remedies. "... maybe I'm gonna be some kind of healer."

Rosemary looked at her older friend with admiration. "Can I learn too?"

Ashley smiled. "Sure! But we'll have to learn mostly from books. The way I see it, hospitals and all their fancy machines and expensive pills aren't going to be around much longer, at least for people like us who do yard work and clean cat boxes for a living ..."

The other 3 burst out laughing. Ashley smiled and waited.

"So all we're gonna have," she continued, "is herbs and simple chemicals, like in that pharmacopeia book, and the stuff we make from them at home."

In the silence that followed, Jeremy wore a frown. Ashley looked at him.

"You might need to hurry," he said. "Our health insurance, from my dad's last job, just ended."

✳

If energy and other resources continue to run low, many careers that young adults dream about will become very rare. Astronauts, pilots, and truck drivers will be hurt by high fuel prices. Manufacturing, retail, and service professions need a growing economy. Firemen, police, and teachers need governments with money to spend.

Young adults, who see the future coming, might want to pursue *two* career paths: one that is their fondest dream, and another they're sure will be around, even in hard times.

In a low-resource world, anything to do with food production will be a winner. Making and repairing simple tools and machines also has a future. Health care, that can work with local resources, will be very important. Can you think of others?

Medicine

Modern medicine expects patients to take little responsibility for their health, but funnels vast amounts of money to huge corporations for machines and drugs that extend the human life-span. In a world getting poorer because of scarce resources, that medical system may soon cease to be available to most people.

Although we hate "rationing" medical care by saying what the patient can and can't have, we willingly do it by saying who gets medical care and who doesn't. People with money and power will most likely continue to get modern medical care.

For the rest of us, a vast body of knowledge awaits, gathered by the ancient Greeks, the Persians, the Chinese, and many other cultures, right into the 20th century. The plant kingdom creates, free for the picking, millions of bio-chemicals that have "pharmaceutical properties." The Earth gives us some additional chemicals, bees make wax, and animals provide a few more useful things (in addition to food).

Always know your herbs and chemical before using them for *anything*. The medical profession has a monopoly, and intends to keep it, even when they "ration" medical care, so that means us little people must only care for each other informally, among friends, never as a business, and never for pay.

If modern medicine ceases to be available to us, we will probably have to be content with shorter life-spans. Some diseases, that are curable today, will become incurable again. But whatever medical care we have will be available in our communities, and not controlled by huge corporations and far-away governments.

*

Styptic — the pharmaceutical property of contracting tissue and checking bleeding.

Shepherd's Purse — Capsella bursa-pastoris, also called cocowort, pick-pocket, Saint James' weed, toywort. Styptic, astringent, antidiarrheal, stimulant, antiseptic, vulnerary, diuretic, antiscorbutic.

Ascorbic Acid — $C_6H_8O_6$ — vitamin C. Preservative, antibiotic, antiscorbutic. From currants, rose hips, citrus fruits, tomatoes, peppers, papayas, guavas, dark-green vegetables ...

New Team Members?

"Tell us about your cousin," Ashley said to Rosemary after enjoying a golden-brown toasted marshmallow.

"He's 14, has goats and a donkey, wants a horse someday. He hikes and camps and everything, and I bet he'd be good on our team. Lives on Kelly Road."

"So he could ride his bike here," Bobby speculated.

"Yeah."

Jeremy squirmed a little. "Does he have a ... girlfriend?"

"I don't think so."

Jeremy frowned, but Ashley didn't notice.

"Any objections to Rosemary seeing what he thinks about preparing?" Ashley asked the entire team.

Rosemary and Bobby shook their heads. Jeremy was silent, so Ashley nodded at Rosemary.

"Okay," Rosemary agreed with a proud smile. "I think I'll see him next Wednesday."

Ashley put another marshmallow on her stick. "You had someone too, right Bobby?"

"Yeah. Girl in my church, Chelsea, 9 years old I think, but really grown up for her age. Takes the bus and goes shopping by herself and stuff. Her dad's a banker, says the world's a real mess ..."

"We *knew* that!" Rosemary interrupted.

Bobby grinned and nodded. "The Sunday-school teacher changes the subject any time Chelsea tries to say anything about it."

"Figures," Jeremy said under his breath.

"Any objection to Bobby seeing what she thinks?" Ashley asked.

"A little young," Jeremy said, "but as long as you think she's grown up enough, go for it."

Bobby nodded.

Ashley was silent as she rotated her marshmallow near the fire. Finally she took a slow, thoughtful breath. "Our team is ... really great ... and I want to be super-careful about new people."

Jeremy raised his eyebrows. "Remember when you thought Bobby was too young and would ruin the team?"

Ashley squirmed. "Yeah. I was wrong. But that doesn't mean just *anyone* will work."

"Agreed," Jeremy said, and the other 2 nodded.

Your Growing Team

We've already talked about the tricky question of adults on your team. Perhaps an "outer team" could include your supportive parents, a neighbor, and a cool teacher, and the "inner team" would be just you and your friends. After all, most grown-ups aren't very comfortable at a campfire or in a tree house.

You should probably keep your team small. More than about 8 people, and you'll get "political factions" that will work against trust and cooperation. It's just a normal part of human nature, and isn't your fault.

Equal numbers of boys and girls? Both have important survival skills, with boys leaning toward machines and animals, and girls toward gardens and medicine. The future certainly needs both. A significant imbalance could cause "games" that would keep your team from being a comfortable place.

Some groups try to avoid those "games" by only having one gender.

A balance of "brain" and "brawn" (muscle)? In our story, Ashley is a bit more "brawn" (and leadership), and Jeremy's the "brain."

Conservative or liberal? Those labels change too quickly to have any importance to a survival team. Political leaders vote for something one year, rant against it the next. "Conserving" valuable supplies and knowledge, and making use of the "liberty" we have to prepare for what's coming, are certainly both good values. Survival is not a political fad.

Everyone close in age, or open to whoever's interested? The author has known 7-year-olds who could handle it, but for average people, 12-ish is about the minimum. There is, of course, no upper age limit on people who are *not* grown up enough.

But true "children" (of any age) shouldn't be on your team. There's nothing wrong with having fun while you prepare. But if you have fun *instead* of preparing, then you will remain unprepared.

Your team, however, should be aware of the children in your families, and others who live nearby, because you might be the only people able to care for them in a crisis. Knowing now what they're like (helpful, passive, defiant) and what special needs they have (medical, vision, hearing, allergies) will make it easier if that situation arises.

A Team of 5?

Rosemary's hot dog was burnt to a crisp before she noticed. Her friends could see she was upset.

Ashley scooted close and put her arm around the 12-year-old. "Your cousin?"

Rosemary's eyes glistened with tears. "He laughed at me! Said he was going to make a million dollars breeding race horses, and computers would do all the work."

Jeremy snickered. "That's what my little brother thinks. Then he yells for me every time his computer crashes."

"Scratch Rosemary's cousin off the list!" Ashley asserted. "Just hearing that he laughed at her was all I need to know. You have any better luck, Bobby?"

"Yeah. Chelsea was cool about it, says her parents already have a deep pantry, but is worried because her dad still has most of their money in stocks and bonds and other stuff I don't understand. She's gonna talk to her parents and thinks they'll let her ride her bike over here alone during the day — it's about a mile — but not at night."

"I could ride with her home after campfires," Ashley said.

Jeremy nodded, but Rosemary looked thoughtful. "What are we gonna do if people, like my cousin, all of a sudden want to join our team when things get really bad?"

"You mean if his dream of making a million dollars doesn't work out?" Jeremy asked with a grin.

Rosemary chuckled, nodded, and wiped the last of her tears onto a sleeve.

The circle of friends became silent as the fire continued to softly crackle.

"That's a huge question," Ashley finally said. "I don't know the answer about any certain person. We'd have to make that decision together, as a team. But I do know something."

Jeremy looked at her with curiosity and respect.

"We're not a refugee camp," Ashley began. "You know how hard it was just to get our parents to accept that we're always welcome at each other's houses. Jeremy's got half a deep pantry, and the rest of us have barely begun. We can't save the whole world — today, tomorrow, or next year."

Farewell to the Team

One cold autumn evening by the campfire, the team talked for more than an hour about a bunch of really bad economic news that was all over the internet, even getting into the main-stream news.

Jeremy seemed especially thoughtful, and the others wondered if it was because his dad was still out of work.

Suddenly, he surprised everyone by scooting over close to Ashley and putting his arm around her.

Ashley couldn't help but tense up, as she had never before felt the emotions that were now making her heart race and her skin tingle.

Feeling her tension, and getting no other reaction, Jeremy's courage faded and he pulled his arm back.

A dozen conflicting thoughts and images flashed into Ashley's mind. The cute boy on the football team smiled at her, even though he had never looked at her in real life. A sports car, with a well-dressed guy at the wheel, skidded to a stop right beside her, but cheer leaders jumped in before Ashley could imagine how to respond. A clean-cut young man in a business suit winked at her, then stepped into a Wall Street bank just as the pillars started crumbling. The boy at school, whose father owned a mill, grinned seductively, then cracked a whip at his hundreds of workers.

After what seemed like forever, but was just a few moments as the fire softly crackled, she saw someone else in her mind's eye. Her friend Jeremy was carefully packing his go-bag, stocking his deep pantry, reading an old book on bicycle repair, and pushing his lawn mower at Mrs. Green's house. He wasn't quite as cute as the other boys, certainly not as well-dressed or rich, but her heart told her it was time to do something ... about her future.

She took a deep breath and gently grabbed Jeremy's arm. "Wait! Would you ... put that back ... where it was ... please?"

Time stood still as the slight frown on Jeremy's face melted, and his arm timidly crept back toward Ashley.

This time she managed to not tense up, and after a moment, smiled slightly as she gazed into the dancing flames of the campfire.

Rosemary and Bobby looked at each other and shrugged.

Closing Thoughts

Why would the story of Ashley's team end with a romantic moment?

Because preparing to survive the changes happening in the world, in 2012 and beyond, isn't just playing some little game or simulation. Nor is it preparation for "The End of the World" (a world with no future).

The chances of something happening that would "end the world" are so slight, they're not worth thinking about. What looks almost *certain* is that our world is going through some big changes, and if we have our eyes open, and we're prepared, we'll change with it.

In the process of surviving the years ahead, most young adults will also find yourselves called by the basic instincts of all living creatures: to secure your home and food supply, and to find companionship and love.

During good times, when society doesn't have

much else to do, it likes to make complicated rules about all those basic "home-making" instincts.

Building codes tell us what we can build. The accepted designs assume cheap and plentiful energy. The rules prohibit, or make more difficult, anything experimental or "home-made."

Relationship and marriage laws assume that parents are employed, public schools will baby-sit you until you're 18, and then a job or college will await you.

As you (hopefully) are aware, many of those assumptions are becoming unreliable.

Society, in the meantime, is starting to be distracted with bigger issues as global economic and political systems go through huge changes (some people would say, "crash and burn"). That will leave us "little people" more freedom to figure out the rules of life for ourselves.

That might seem scary, but it's actually a good thing. The old rules may not work much longer, and we may need to invent new rules. I cannot foresee what those rules will be. You are smart and strong, or you wouldn't be interested in preparing for the future, and that future will soon be in your hands.

As you step into the future, remember to hope, but not for things the world can no longer give. Hope for what you have the power to find: happiness in everything you do, minute by minute, year by year.

Master Checklist

To make it easier to find the relevant chapter, this list
is in the same order as the ideas appear in the book.

Decision: to be prepared
Go-Bag
    Wallet/purse, emergency money, ID, numbers
    Shoes/boots, socks, coat
    Water/juice, food
    First-Aid, toiletries, glasses, medicine
    Other stuff
Team!
Analysis: medium probability & severity dangers
Deep Pantry
    Non-perishable staple foods
    Cooking adjuncts: oil, baking powder, spices ...
    Drinking water, wash water supply
    Alternate cooking fuel
    Comfort foods and "lullabies"
Practice: turning basic food into an edible meal

Medical

First-Aid and CPR training

Robust family medical kit

Books

Analysis: involvement of parents and other adults

Web of Life

Present

Future

Discussion: which goals can be blocked

Analysis: your happiness

Doing Business

Birth certificate, state ID card, passport

Practice: money orders, mail-order purchases

Discussion: possible hunting/trapping gear

Practice: emotional resilience

Discussion: myths and fallacies

Practice: earning money

Casual labor

Value adding

Bartering

Good community reputation

Invisibility

Analysis: unintended enemy/criminal appearance

Analysis: assets that might be "magnets"

Discussion: situations to avoid with "invisibility"

Practice: territorial avoidance and "invisibility"

Discussion: behaviors, colors, accessories

Discussion: lifeboat ethics

The Future
  Analysis: electricity and gasoline prices x2, x10
  Discussion: avoiding effects of empire decline
  Discussion: future trends and their effects
Practice: useful news sources
Meeting/message places
Money and Wealth
  Money storage at home
  Practice: dealing with banks, cashing checks
  Analysis: personal and family debts
  Discussion: your primary wealth
  Silver (and maybe gold) coins
Deep Preparation
  Analysis: survivability of your home, alternates
  Practice: voluntary poverty (backpacking, etc.)
  Get to know your "Reptile" and your "Angel"
  Practice: good boundaries
  Practice: reality levels of problems/solutions
Some Touchy Issues
  Analysis: "lullabies" you use or misuse
  Discussion: avoiding refugee status
  Analysis: available religions in your area
  Discussion: educating the next generation
  Analysis: your career goals (dream, practical)
More Team Thoughts
  Discussion: other people to let on your team
  Analysis: family and neighborhood children
Personal analysis: relationships in your future

About the Author

Born in the Mojave Desert, J. Z. Colby now lives and writes deep in a forest of the Pacific Northwest.

He has studied many subjects, formally and informally, including psychology, philosophy, education, and performing arts, but remains a generalist. His primary profession as a mental health counselor, specializing with families and young adults, gives him many stories of personal growth, and the motivation to develop his team of young critiquers and readers.

All his life, he has been drawn toward a broad understanding of human nature, especially those physical, emotional, mental, and spiritual situations in which our capacity to function seems to reach its limits. He finds fascinating those few individuals who can transcend the limits of our common human nature and the dictates of our cultures.

In his spare time, he flies helicopters and airplanes.

He may be contacted at the email address listed on the internet site www.nebador.com.

www.ingramcontent.com/pod-product-compliance
Lightning Source LLC
Chambersburg PA
CBHW021152020426
42331CB00003B/28